Walking by Faith While Living in Pain

Walking by Faith While Living in Pain

A Christian Deals With Suffering

Thomas L. Endicott

Pathway Press

Unless otherwise indicated, Scripture quotations are taken from the *New King James Version*. Copyright © 1979, 1980, 1982, 1990, 1995, Thomas Nelson Inc., Publishers.

Scriptures marked KJV are from the King James Version of the Bible.

Scripture quotations marked *NIV* are taken from the Holy Bible, *New International Version®*. Copyright © 1973, 1978, 1984 by International Bible Society. Used by permission of Zondervan Publishing House. All rights reserved.

Scripture quotations marked *Amp*. Are from *The Amplified Bible*. Old Testament copyright © 1965, 1987 by the Zondervan Corporation. *The Amplified New Testament* copyright © 1958, 1987 by the Lockman Foundation. Used by permission.

Scripture quotations marked *TM* are from *The Message*. Copyright © 1993. Used by permission of NavPress Publishing Group.

God's Word® is a copyrighted work of God's Word to the Nations. Quotations are used by permission. Copyright 1995 by God's Word to the Nations. All rights reserved.

Scripture quotations marked *NASB* are taken from the *New American Standard Bible®*. Copyright © The Lockman Foundation 1960, 1962, 1963, 1968, 1971, 1972, 1973, 1975, 1977. Used by permission.

Book Editor: Wanda Griffith
Editorial Assistant: Tammy Hatfield
Copy Editors: Esther Metaxas
Julie E. McGuire

Library of Congress Catalog Card Number: 2005908251
ISBN: 1-59684-123-0
Copyright © 2005 by Pathway Press
Cleveland, Tennessee 37311
All Rights Reserved
Printed in the United States of America

DEDICATION

To

Ann...

who has been by my side as a loving wife for 38 years.

She embodies the portion of the wedding covenant that states, "in sickness and in health, for richer for poorer, for better for worse."

Her abiding love and care have given us a home of peace, which is centered on our faith.

CONTENTS

Acknowledgments 9

Foreword 11

Introduction 13

Chapter 1
    Pain and Faith—an Oxymoron? 15

Chapter 2
    What You Cannot See Is Healable 31

Chapter 3
    Lord, It Hurts! 43

Chapter 4
    Is Something Wrong With My Faith? 57

Chapter 5
    How Long Will It Last? 71

Chapter 6
    Why Am I So Depressed? 83

Chapter 7
    I Can't Let Go 97

Chapter 8
    My Loved One Died! 107

Chapter 9
    I Have Met Job's Friends 121

Chapter 10
    His Burden, My Blessing 131

Chapter 11
    Some of My Heroes 143

Chapter 12
    I Am Not a Loser 157

Chapter 13
    Becoming a Better Person Through Suffering ... 169

Chapter 14
    Acceptance Must Be in My Vocabulary! 181

Chapter 15
    Walking Faith 191

Chapter 16
    How Do I Affect Those Around Me? 205

Chapter 17
    Never, Never, Never Give Up! 215

Acknowledgments

An artist may consider the painting his own, yet he received inspiration from someone or something. Another may have framed and displayed his work, and, finally it was purchased.

It is the same with this book.

- My wife and children encouraged me to write.
- My friend, David S. Bishop, added his own experience and wonderful insight.
- Dr. Bill George of Pathway Press and his editorial committee accepted this work for publication.

There are the designers and artists who give the book its character and the printing staff that gives the book life.

To these and you who have chosen to purchase *Walking by Faith While Living in Pain*, I am thankful and deeply moved.

Ultimately, my greatest praise of thankfulness is to my Savior and Lord for His wisdom, encouragement and insight.

God bless you all is my prayer.

Foreword

Pain is no stranger to any of us. For some pain is occasional, for some it is intermittent, and for some it is chronic. No matter who we are or what we believe, at times we will be confronted by pain.

Theologically, pain poses a problem to many. Some will wonder why a good God allows it. They seem to ignore the far-reaching ramifications of the fallen, sinful condition of the world in which we live. Others will ponder why at times it persists in light of Scriptural promises. While all of us have experienced pain in varying forms, many of us have also experienced times when its power has been divinely broken and its persistence alleviated. So . . . what can a person do when caught in the tension between the reality of persistent pain and the prayerful longing for its release?

If I am confronted by a problem and I am looking for help, I go to a resource that is valid. I seek out a person who not only understands my situation from an objective point of view, but one who has experienced my predicament and can give me practical advice that is going to help. The person who has experienced my situation identifies with me and that is valuable. When I also discover that he has struggled with a situation like mine and has come to practical guidelines for resolution, that is empowering. That's what I am looking for. That really helps.

As you read this book, you will find just that kind of help and hope. Tom Endicott has walked through the valley of pain and has not lost his faith in God's goodness nor His power to do the impossible. I have known Tom for many years. We worked together for several years and have been friends for a long time. I know of the grievous nature of the pain-filled valley through which he has walked and of the many surgeries he has undergone. I have been there for some of them. Tom is not an ivory-towered idealist who only projects strategies, but a bloodied soldier from the front lines of the painful conflict. So, when he talks about faith . . . he knows firsthand what God can do. He has great faith. But when he talks about persistent pain, he deals with practical issues that not only make suggestions but also bring fulfillment.

Tom talks about the pain he has experienced in a straightforward manner. In looking at the ramifications of it, he doesn't dodge tough questions. He believes life should be lived productively and triumphantly and, as one who has been through it, he shows how. He speaks to theological issues with insight and to practical matters with wisdom and helpfulness. To deal with all of these facets is challenging, and yet that is exactly what Tom sets out to do . . . and he succeeds.

To that person seeking help for a painful situation, you will find help in this book.

—Reverend David S. Bishop, Ph.D.

Introduction

Following a service in which my subject had been on faith, a dear lady asked me, "How can you preach on faith when you are not healed?" In a few words, she defined the theme of this work. Can faith and illness coexist comfortably in today's Christian community of thought and literature?

Many will have a negative reply to this question, while others will quietly try to ignore this uncomfortable theological situation. Some will be stoutly resolute regarding their position of faith and those who are not healed. This simply states, "If you have enough faith, nothing is impossible, and your healing is assured." Another form of this answer may be, "If you quote these scriptures and pray this prayer, you will be healed." There are various combinations of answers, but they ultimately may be summarized that with the correct faith, healing will occur.

Where does this leave those with birth defects, blinded eyes and crippled bodies who are faithful believers yet have not received their healing? There are thousands of people with chronic illnesses and terminal diseases that may feel like second-class Christians because they have not had their miracle of healing. These struggle daily just to have some type of a normal life. How would Helen Keller have responded to those who might question her faith and walk with Christ?

These questions and more are addressed within these pages. You may see your own health and faith situation and finally be able to say, "I can live with this." On the other hand, you might find your own sense of worth and self-esteem restored as you realize that you are not alone and God has not given up on you. If you are a caregiver, you too will find that you are needed and loved.

This multifaceted approach to faith and pain seeks to satisfy the troubled soul and bring new joy to the believer. Instead of solely seeking theological explanations to the issue of chronic pain and illness, this text will supply practical solutions.

This book does not seek to disprove those who teach or follow the "word of faith" movement, but it seeks to find the smooth road to a balanced walk with our Lord. We rejoice with those who are healed miraculously and celebrate those who have faced life's hardships and retained their love for Him. Regardless of your personal life in Christ, you will be lifted up and encouraged to go on.

The theme of this writing comes from this verse: "Finally, brethren, whatever things are true, whatever things are noble, whatever things are just, whatever things are pure, whatever things are lovely, whatever things are of good report, if there is any virtue and if there is anything praiseworthy—meditate on these things" (Philippians 4:8).

I pray that you will be richly blessed and ministered to while reading *Walking by Faith While Living in Pain*.

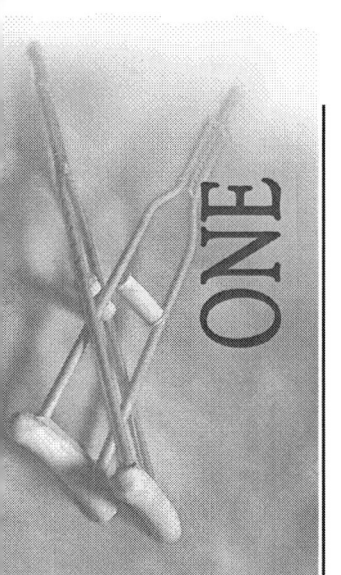

ONE

Pain and Faith—an Oxymoron?

"But the fruit of the Spirit is love, joy, peace, longsuffering, gentleness, goodness, faith, meekness, temperance: against such there is no law" (Galatians 5:22, 23, KJV).

Pain and faith don't go together . . . why?

Most readers know what an oxymoron is. For those in doubt, it is a rhetorical figure in which incongruous or contradictory terms are combined, as in *a deafening silence* and *turkey ham*. A classic illustration of an oxymoron is *jumbo shrimp*. Jumbo refers to something large, whereas a shrimp refers to something small. One of my favorites is *an educated guess*.

Why would I start a book about an oxymoron? To be blunt, recent generations of Christians are very careful not to use the words *pain* and *faith* together. Yet many have found faith in the midst of pain. However, very few people would describe faith and pain as existing together at ease. They will find personal discomfort in believing that those who are disabled, ill, or racked with pain have a level of faith that depicts their understanding of Christ and His healing power or greater will.

We have heard promises of physical healing and monetary prosperity to all who verbalize their wishes. Teaching that words of "positive confession" will move God and He will grant our wishes has been common and widely accepted.

Before I go further, I want to establish a common ground of understanding. I believe faith is what pleases God. We are healed by the stripes of Christ; miracles still do occur, and God is sovereign.

Why do people say you do not have enough faith?

A sad tragedy occurs when Christians measure faith by worldly prosperity or good health. Therefore, when they come across someone who is ill, they claim it is because this person "must not have enough faith." They think their success is evidence that their faith is strong and the proof is their good health or prosperity.

If we had their faith, we would not be sick; thus, those of us who are suffering are somehow afflicted because we lack willpower, fortitude and attitude that supply our faith. Look to the scripture that started this chapter. The fruit of the Spirit inhabits each Christian. Long-suffering means fortitude and it is only one portion of the fruit. Other portions, such as love, joy, peace, gentleness and goodness, reflect our attitude. It is our attitude during times of pain and trials that makes a greater difference, not only to the one suffering, but also to those around them.

Will faith cause the pain to leave?

Pain is universal. I have yet to see a person hit his or her thumb with a hammer or stub a toe without saying "ouch" or giving a muffled grunt sound. Was there a lack of faith involved because they suffered pain? Of course not, they just proved that they are human.

When a hammer hits a thumb, the one thing we all want is for the throbbing to stop as soon as possible. We are universal in our reactions to pain. I remember watching a young boy putting Christmas lights around a small tree outside his house. He was standing in wet snow and the lights did not come on. In an effort to test the wiring, he unscrewed a bulb and stuck his wet finger in the socket. I can see him today, jumping up and down saying, "What to do, what to do." It was a strange reaction, but then again, response to pain from any source is "make it go away."

So the big question is, "If I have pain, is there something wrong with my faith?" It all depends upon what I have faith in—a person, theory, object, formula or supplier of faith. I am amused by fads or waves that seem to move through churches. These people require a change in their spiritual meal plan, or they move on to another church where "it is happening." Often, these waves cause confusion and wrong ideas about faith, pain and healing.

A few years ago, one particular spiritual group believed and taught that the devil and demons were behind all pain and malady. I was at a gathering of families in the movement and we had finished eating lunch. A young man had just fed his baby who was crying. He began shaking his finger at his

2-month-old, and in silence casting out demons when the child burped. Daddy then had a very pleased look on his face because he had been taught that when a demon leaves, there is a physical manifestation.

As a father of three, it was not hard for me to realize that his baby had gas and needed to be burped. I shook my head in dismay and made that my last meeting with that group.

What if it will not go away when I pray?

In 1998, I awoke one morning and got out of my bed. I fell on my face in excruciating pain. I silently prayed for relief, but every movement just increased pain. Somehow, my wife was able to get me to my workplace. I was compelled to go because my friend had just been named director of my department and I did not want to let him down. He prayed. Others gathered around and prayed, but there was no release from pain. An ambulance was called and I was shuttled between two hospitals before a doctor said he could help me. The problem had been from a previous lumbar surgery. Five out of six pedicle screws were loose and fusion material had disappeared.

Before a surgical solution was found, my wife, my pastor and I had prayed for relief, but it would not come. I know there are many who have experienced an accident or disease where, in spite of prayer, medication was all that would relieve the pain. I did not give up on God, and if you are reading this book, you doubtless did not either. You understood that God intervenes in His time, place and way. You did not consider God to be a failure or His Word to be in error. You trusted in your faith that was given to you at conversion and has grown with spiritual maturity.

Does He hear my prayers?

> *The Christian life is not a constant high.*
> *I have my moments of deep discouragement.*
> *I have to go to God in prayer with tears in my eyes, and say,*
> *'O God, forgive me,' or 'Help me.'*
>
> —Billy Graham

There are many times when it feels as though our prayers just bounce off the ceiling. It is easy to wonder if God, in fact, does hear. Imagine millions of people around our world who are petitioning God for health, finances, family and friends. Is it conceivable that any person or being is able to personally assimilate and answer each of the millions of prayers? These requests are not just in millions but also in millions per second, day in and day out.

Thank goodness, God does not operate within human limitations. He is able to identify each prayer, relate it to a person contextually, know the proper answer and reply individually. His nature is love, but He is omniscient, omnipotent and omnipresent.

I love a song called "Someone to Care," by Jimmy Davis. Here is the chorus:

> Someone to care, someone to share,
> All your troubles like no other can do.

He'll come down from the skies and brush the tears from your eyes.
You're His child and He cares for you.

Why won't it go away when others have prayed?

Discouragement may set in after a gifted person has prayed for you. The latest and greatest evangelist has prayed; your pastor and every staff member, church choir and soundman have prayed for you, yet you are still ill and in pain. I have had some evangelists pray in silence, while others yelled, slapped my back or hit my head. Still the pain remained. Others who attended special seminars have spoken many different prayers, manipulated my spine or tickled my ribs. Their answer was always that something was wrong with me because I was not healed.

I have a prayer group and support group—what else will it take?

No doubt, we have all known a desperately ill person. Often friends, neighbors and church members form a special support group for the person. Regardless of the efforts of all, the ill person died. Who failed? Did the person not have enough faith, or did a member of the support group not believe as strongly as others? These difficult, but common, situations cause us to struggle with our faith.

Meanwhile, there will be times as previously mentioned, when an ill person is healed miraculously. We all rejoice at their healing, and believe with strengthened attitudes, that we can do it again. A problem with this is that we cannot formulate ways to bring healing to people. When we examine ourselves, we want things to happen, as we desire and at a proper time.

Starting a car engine is an example. When you get in your car, you fasten your seat belt, turn the ignition key, and expect to hear a motor start. If the starter just grinds and grinds, or clicks without starting, most people find their satisfaction level decreased because of an unfulfilled expectation. Results are good expectations, whereas failures are bad expectations. Who wants to be disappointed?

Why am I not pleasing God?

How depressing it must be for the infirm, maimed and disabled to hear statements such as a leading "faith movement" teacher made: "How can you glorify God in your body, when it doesn't function right? What makes you think the Holy Ghost wants to live inside of a body where He can't see out through the windows, and He can't hear out the ears?"[1]

It is a disservice to those who were born without sight or hearing to say they are not pleasing to God. Helen Keller would indeed disagree with the statement. She proved that being blind, deaf and mute were not hindrances to a fruitful life.

Optimism is the faith that leads to achievement. Nothing can be done without hope or confidence.
—Helen Keller

Is God testing me?

I was fortunate to have wonderful grandparents. My paternal grandfather died when I was young; however, my maternal grandfather had a great influence in my life. He never had much money, but he had many friends. Grandpa was never angry, but he always had a nickel in his pocket to buy me a candy bar or toy airplane. He taught me about God and my Bible. As I grew, I learned to relate to God through my grandfather's traits of love and charity. He and my grandmother raised an autistic young man to adulthood as if he was their own.

When I was 18, Grandpa developed pancreatic cancer. I would care for him when I was home on leave from Maine Maritime Academy. As I changed his bandages and irrigated his drain tube, though in pain, he never uttered an unkind word. The last time I saw him alive, he said, "My God is testing me."

I drove away from his hospital asking God why He would let such a wonderful man suffer. At once, I understood that Grandpa was not complaining, but praising God. To Grandpa, God took pleasure in him enough to let him know that He was there even in pain. My grandfather accepted it as a reward, not a test of will and faithfulness. Grandpa's death was very serene, and we all sang his favorite hymn at his funeral, "Nearer My God to Thee."

❝ *The problem is not that there are problems.*
   The problem is expecting otherwise
      and thinking that having problems is a problem. ❞
                              —Theodore Rubin

What did I do to deserve this?

One of our first questions is "Why?" whether responding to the death of a loved one or to a tragic accident. It is our nature to desire explanations for what is happening to others and us. No one wants to go to a doctor and hear the words: "I do not know." We expect the same of spiritual leaders. These people have studied and made their life's work a means for helping others. They must have a definitive answer.

The truth is that no matter how well-educated and experienced, we cannot always expect an answer that will satisfy. Yes, doctors can explain the physiology of the body and its reaction to accidents and illness; however, why it happens is not always clear. Perhaps a person's lifestyle has led to current illness while others develop a similar illness but have lived a different mode of life.

I know of young people who were killed in automobile accidents while on their way to or from ministry functions. They were not at fault; they were not driving recklessly, yet they were plucked from their parents in an instance. Tragedy without visible or personal benefits can or may affect us all. What role is faith playing in the midst of great emotional pain? I will address this issue later in the text.

When my wife and I had been married three years, we decided it was time to start a family. Our daughter was born only to die two hours later. I signed her birth and death certificate at the same time. We asked our doctor why, and he did not have a good explanation. Nevertheless, he told us that there was no reason why we should not have children in our future.

A year later, my wife was on a stretcher wheeling out of a delivery room and all she could do was to hold up two fingers indicating twins. I was overjoyed and remarked, "God has given us back the one we lost." They had been born prematurely, and one had hyaline membrane disease, or neonatal respiratory distress syndrome (RDS). This occurs in a premature baby's lungs—60 percent incidence in infants born at less than 28 weeks' gestation. Our doctor told me that we might be taking one child home. Little Baby B was in distress. Hyaline membrane disease had taken the life of President John and Jacqueline Kennedy's child born during his brief presidency, and that historical recollection weighed heavily on me.

That night as I was alone, I begged God not to let us go through the loss of a child again. I still believe that my first reaction of God giving us back our loss was pleasing to Him. Five days later, Baby B was going to make it, but then Baby A was in trouble. He had severe apnea, and a nurse had to sit continually by his incubation unit and give him a gentle snap with her finger to start his breathing. That was in 1971, and preemies like ours did not have available the great equipment and skills now possessed by pediatric medicine. It was another two weeks before Baby A could breathe without stimulus.

I was not a devout believer in those days, but my upbringing from youth had never caused me to doubt God. I just did not know Him. After six weeks, we joyously brought two very small babies home to a one-bedroom apartment.

As a side note, we were told that Baby A might be blind and Baby B would have breathing difficulties the rest of his life. Both are now career officers in the Navy and U.S. Air Force. Four years later, my wife delivered a healthy, happy baby girl. Our family was complete."

Did we or others like us deserve what happened? Again, the answer is no. Let this scripture answer: "But they that wait upon the Lord shall renew their strength; they shall mount up with wings as eagles; they shall run, and not be weary; and they shall walk, and not faint" (Isaiah 40:31, KJV).

Why is my loved one going through this?

I firmly believe that caregivers are the greatest, though often the least appreciated, people in the world. They take care of a child, parents, husband or wife through a terminal illness, recovery or ongoing disability, which requires sacrificing their time, pleasures and often their personal health.

For example, consider a woman caring for her husband with Alzheimer's disease. Often, her husband is past his 50s, and all their married life he has been a virile and robust man. Now, she watches him decline little by little from the man she married to a person who eventually will not even recognize her. Emotional pain is definite, and times of helplessness will come. At present, there is no cure for Alzheimer's, and who could blame a caregiver for feeling hopeless?

As a tremendous aid, there are support groups who help caregivers work through those feelings without condemnation. They may also have their local church and neighbors for support. The Alzheimer's Foundation of America focuses on "Together for Care . . . in Addition to Cure." Their Web site is *www.alzfdn.org*. There are multiple Web sites available when searching for Alzheimer's disease.

It is never easy to watch a loved one progress through a terminal disease. Many sons and daughters have watched their parents die from cancer and have asked why they are going through such suffering and pain. I was with both of my parents when they died. It hurts to watch them slowly move toward death, but I would stay with them and quietly quote the Psalms. It always appeared that the Twenty-third Psalm was most comforting for them.

I have listed all the scriptures on healing, why am I still not healed?

The pastor of our church has compiled a booklet containing scriptures related to healing. He receives many requests for his booklet—more than ever when someone becomes ill. Reading Scripture is soothing and encouraging.

When a member of our former church was dying, my wife gathered the same scriptures and typed them into a notebook for her to read. The member also had a strong support group, each of whom had the same scriptures. When the group came to her home, they would read scriptures and pray together. They all had a strong belief that she would be healed, but in the end, she passed away.

Had the person, group or scriptures failed? Once again, the answer is no. "We are assured and know that [God being a partner in their labor] all things work together and are [fitting into a plan] for good to and for those who love God and are called according to [His] design and purpose" (Romans 8:28, *Amp.*).

Not all things are necessarily good. I have yet to get excited and shout with glee when I get a flat tire. My good "things" are a spare tire in my trunk that is full of air and a working jack. A flat tire was not good. But because I had been certain I was ready for an emergency, all the "things" worked for good.

Even though a person has read and listened to scriptures, such acts do not guarantee pain and sickness will go away. A good characteristic is that they are being faithful and trusting that God's will is perfect and everything will work out for His good. Maybe it is not what is expected, but it is difficult to see an end when you are in the midst of a trial.

The apostle Paul describes faith in Hebrews 11:1 (*GW*): "Faith assures us of things we expect and convinces us of the existence of things we cannot see." This verse may be paraphrased to read: "Faith is the ability to see into the world of spirits, invisible and eternal. It is the power to understand those things which are not apparent by natural senses."

Endnote

[1] Price, Fred, *Is God Glorified Through Sickness?*, audio tape # FP605

Reflections for Discussion

1. What conflicts or agreements arise when the author states that pain and faith do not exist together comfortably?

2. Do some people measure faith by worldly prosperity or good health?

3. Does all pain come from demonic sources or is some pain natural?

4. Are you able to conceive of God's abilities, especially omniscience?

5. How difficult is it to see God's goodness while suffering personally or while watching a loved one nearing death?

TWO

What You Cannot See Is Healable

"*When a faith-healer commands God to perform a miracle, in the absence of a prayer that says, 'Thy will be done,' it is, as far as I am concerned, the most rank form of arrogance... The faith-healer Bosworth once said that faith makes God act. If you follow that line of reasoning God is in His heaven, but Bosworth rules the world!*"

—C. Everett Koop, retired U.S. Surgeon General

Who can be healed?

I have noted over the years that some people believe if an illness or pain-causing injury is not visible, then it can be healed through faith. A person whose legs have been removed due to diabetes, or someone with a hand missing because of an accident, is often accepted "as is." However, it would be correct to pray for someone with diabetes and seek the Lord for healing of this disease that ravages his or her body. When meeting a person with an illness or painful condition who appears outwardly healthy, one response may be to tell them to hang in there... they are going to be all right. Another common response is, "I will pray for you." This reply may be truthful, but many merely make this as an empty gesture, leaving the person who is ill feeling unwanted and neglected.

On a beautiful summer day in New England, we were playing softball at a church picnic. Teens and adults played, along with the younger children under a parent's care. During our game, a batter took a hard swing at a pitch but lost his grip on the bat. It flew directly toward other team members on the sideline and hit a young teenage girl in her forehead, splitting her forehead with a dreadful gash. I grabbed our First Aid kit and applied pressure to her injury. While others prayed, I gave instructions for someone to call for transportation to an emergency room. Thankfully, she simply required stitches and her scar is hidden in her hair. It could have been worse, but I believe that this incident showed practical Christianity. Just as the injured man on the Jericho Road was nursed by the "Good Samaritan" and given a room in which to recover, our church group ministered first aid to the girl, prayer and then consolation for the batter. He was very upset that his loss of control had caused her injury. Those were days when people did not sue over accidents, and the incident was soon forgotten.

How do we answer others when healing doesn't come?

For more than 25 years, I have been in constant pain from spinal stenosis, nerve damage and continuing arthritic deformities. I have had 15 major surgeries on my spine with a multitude of ancillary surgeries to aid in pain control. Today, I walk in a bent position and am unable to walk, stand or sit upright for lengthy periods. (Lengthy is considered longer than 10 minutes.) I also survived a double pulmonary embolism and now require oxygen while sleeping.

During these years I have been pastoring, therefore I am more visible. I mention this because I have met well-intentioned people who have given me everything from something that tasted like hay chaff from a barn floor, bee's honey, magnets, copper wrist bands to herbs with more names than the nations they come from. Other people have approached me with special prayers just for spines, formulated gestures and untold words of wisdom that if I would follow, I would be healed. Yet, at this writing, I am facing another major spinal surgery.

During a discussion with a man who was a strong believer in the Word-Faith movement, I asked if there were any situations where prayer would not work. He emphatically answered in the negative. He was trying to convince me that I would be healed if I would believe as he did. I then asked him, if my arm was cut off at my shoulder either due to an accident or birth defect, would he pray for God to grow a new one for me? He answered with an emphatic, "Yes, God can do anything!"

I did not argue with him, and I must agree that God can do anything, though I had serious doubts that I would grow a missing limb. I am reminded of Matthew 14:1-12, which describes the beheading of John the Baptist. Jesus' disciples took John's body, buried it and then they told Jesus. None prayed for John to have a new head or for it to reattach. This previous statement may seem coarse or vulgar; however, it relates well to my supposed missing limb.

Do I want my healing? Yes and amen is my answer. Although it has been during quiet times of recovery in a hospital that I have felt God's presence in a personal manner—not just His love, but a physical touch. Following one surgery, I experienced a near-death situation, which filled me with the peace of God, and after another, I healed faster than expected.

Are there other examples where people of faith weren't healed?

There is a teaching based on our natural desire to live without trial and tribulation, and to live in a type of heaven on earth. "He who dies with the most toys wins." That slogan appeared on T-shirts and hats some time ago. Christians would call that a worldly attitude, but many Christians have fallen into similar traps. They just give it a different name: God's promises, health and prosperity, indicating that if you use correct wording and Scriptures, you can escape afflictions. Second Timothy 4:5 says "But watch thou in all things, endure afflictions, do the work of an evangelist, make full proof of thy ministry."

The word *afflictions* in the previous Scripture is the Greek word *kakopatheo*, which means "to undergo hardship: be afflicted, endure afflictions (hardness), suffer trouble." Even the famous evangelist, Kathryn Kuhlman, known for the gift of healing became ill and suffered hardships during her life. I encourage you to visit her Web site (*www.kathrynkuhlman.com*) and listen to the audio files. My favorite is "Money Isn't Everything." We must always remember her basis of ministry was not healing but salvation of souls.

Many have heard terms *name it and claim it* or facetiously, *blab it and grab it*. Teachers who follow this philosophy are placing emphasis on spoken words of men to activate God to a desired result. Power then is actually in man who has intrinsic formulas to make God move by their will. I read that Jesus said, ". . . nevertheless not my will, but thine, be done" (Luke 22:42, KJV). I have always been careful to remember that I am here to serve God, not for Him to serve me.

If it is true that we should not live with trial and illness, then Billy Graham must not be a true believer. At this writing, he is 86 and suffering from Parkinson's disease, a progressive nervous disorder. He is using a walker while he recuperates after two falls earlier this year that broke his pelvic bone in three places. The voice that thundered with righteousness speaks more softly now.

I have watched Billy Graham's ministry over many years and had the pleasure to be a sponsoring pastor when he came to our city. For me, it has been difficult to watch his health deteriorate and to remember the man that came to my city as compared to the man now. I do know this one thing though, there is nothing wrong with his faith. He based his life on a believing faith and his ministry presented that faith in a Savior. I know of no other man in history who has appeared before more people presenting the gospel of Christ. I am confident that most people feel as I do regarding Reverend Graham.

Why do we treat people with unseen diseases in a different way?

Often, pain of lupus, multiple sclerosis and arthritis exists in a believer without visual evidence. Jesus saw the pain of a man with a withered hand, a hemorrhaging woman and a man with congenital blindness. He healed them, while others ran away from Him. People tend to be inconsistent in relating to a very consistent Savior.

I once heard a minister say that it is God's plan for a believer to die healthy. He was declaring that believers are to live long and healthy lives. When it is time to die, they do it in their sleep. Health encompasses fitness, vigor, viability, rigor, well-being and robustness. I have never known of a healthy person to die. Death comes when our body or a major organ loses its viability, well-being or robustness. People may appear to die in their sleep, but something was not healthy. I am sure that it is a natural tendency to want to escape tribulations, live a prosperous life and gently move into heaven.

There are readers who know of people who were healthy, but died in their sleep. I also know of one. It was my grandmother. After Grandpa died, she was alone, yet in favorable health, and she died peacefully in her sleep. Still something went wrong, whether from a pulmonary embolism or a heart attack. We hope that death will take us in our sleep. However, as a pastor, I have been with many when death arrived, and their death came from disease or trauma. The fact that they did not die healthy or in their sleep, had no effect on their salvation or faith.

How do we respond when healing doesn't happen?

Life does not mean the opposite of vigor, vitality and robustness. It does means your body is well enough to still contain a soul and have a personality. One definition is physical, mental and spiritual experiences that represent existence. It is difficult for us to understand why some people seem to live so well, while others suffer.

I am reminded of a hymn, "Farther Along." "Farther along we'll know all about it. Farther along we'll understand why." I used to struggle with that part of the chorus that says, "Cheer up my brother, live in the sunshine." There was a time of deep emotional disappointment when I entered a church service and heard the hymn being sung. Since then, I look back at that experience as God's way of encouraging me, and I have learned to love that great hymn.

Prior to a scheduled surgery, a prominent church member made this statement, "If our pastor had enough faith, he would not need his upcoming surgery." I heard the statement and did not respond. My wife was within hearing distance and it stirred her, yet she had restraint. Later she told me that faith is what we have been living on these last few years. When there was no food in the cellar of a little church where we were living with three children, a person brought two big bags of fresh cucumbers. It was not much, but it was food. When we would go to our car after an evening church service, we often found food on the hood or on the steps of our living quarters. Faith kept us during a time when we did not have health insurance, a steady salary or a home to live in.

Faith is so much more than things; it is a way of life. It is accepting God's will and direction for your life. It is not saying some words and expecting God to beckon to your call right away. It is a life of prayer, fellowship, service and faithfulness to Him through His Word.

How can I preach on faith if I am not healed?

Following a service in which my topic had been faith, a dear lady asked me, "How can you preach on faith when you are not healed?" I paused for a moment, as her question was valid, then I responded. "My experience neither confirms nor negates the Word of God. It stands on its own." I can still see a perplexed look on her face until understanding came, and she walked away pleased with my answer. Frankly, I was astonished at my answer, but upon reflection, I knew it was true.

That response also helped a neurosurgeon on a follow-up visit to his office after surgery. He questioned his faith and ministry as a doctor. He had been an Army surgeon during the Vietnam era and had seen more pain and suffering than most. I pointed out how fortunate he was to have skills and talent to relieve pain and suffering. No matter what he had experienced, God's Word always proved itself, and his ministry was a gift to many. As we prayed, I could see tears flow as a wonderful doctor found his worth in God once again.

> *The good, the bad, hardship, joy, tragedy, love, and happiness are all interwoven into one indescribable whole that one calls life.*
>
> *You cannot separate the good from the bad, and perhaps there is no need to do so.*
>
> —Jacqueline Bouvier Kennedy Onassis

So, do you believe in prayer and healing?

Two years ago, my wife began experiencing severe leg pain that I recognized as sciatic pain. She had difficulty walking while at work. She would push her wheeled office chair up and down the halls. I was able to procure a wheelchair for her so she could continue to work with less effort.

She had a medical exam, along with X-rays and other diagnostic tests given for disk problems. The X-ray showed a bulging disk with a portion broken off. This was causing pressure on her sciatic nerve, resulting in great pain. I did not want my wife to start down the path of endless surgeries and pain that I suffered.

I prayed day and night for her healing. I pleaded with God to rescue her from surgery. He heard my prayers. A couple weeks after her medical tests, she was examined again. The bulging disk had returned to normal and the separate piece had either reattached to the disk, or her body had absorbed it. So, do I believe in prayer and healing? Yes, prayer coupled with faithfulness is very dear to me.

How does disability fit into God's purposes?

A disabled person is no less a faithful Christian than a person whom the world would consider healthy and fit. The church may be compared to a hospital. Prior to salvation, we are all dead in our sin, but afterwards we have a new life. We are new creatures in Him (2 Corinthians 5:17). However, many suffer the ravages of disease and illness brought on by a prior lifestyle. Major organs may be diseased from acute alcoholism, drug abuse or sexually transmitted diseases. Many suffer personality disorders or depression after conversion.

It is a mature person who recognizes potential in people though they may not display the physical prowess of an Olympic athlete. Joni Eareckson Tada continues to show our world that a broken body does not mean a broken spirit. To the contrary, she has astonished us with her artistry, books, ministry, radio programs and innumerable methods of outreach.

In recent times, we heard of the death of Christopher Reeve. The man we once knew as Superman had become a quadriplegic due to a fall from a horse. Yet he overcame the impossible and directed new films, spoke to millions and showed us that disability does not mean liability.

America has made great strides in recognizing the disabled. Establishing special parking, ramps, vehicles and access to previously unreachable areas in public, shows that our government recognizes their needs. Churches may provide those legislated requirements, but they often miss opportunities to minister to disabled people or include them in ministry. Often, I have found their reaction to be one of concerned pity, rather than active empathy that allows a disabled person to show forth their talents and gifts for ministry.

One situation with a potential for embarrassment occurred when a deaf-mute man came to church with his wife. During service, she would sign the message to him. At the finish of the message and altar call, a woman called from the back of our church, "There is a deaf and dumb spirit here. May I come and cast it out?" I was not preaching that day, but was sitting near the visiting couple. When I heard the woman's request, I responded with a "No!" I looked up the aisle in her direction to see her approaching the couple anyway. I met her and asked her, "Please don't do this." She argued some, but I was firm and she returned to her seat. I went to them and apologized for the incident. The man began to sign and his wife interpreted for me. He said, "It's OK, this happens often." He then added, "I speak in tongues, in my heart." As he tapped his chest indicating his heart, I knew that there was no evil spirit there but a devoted man of God, full of grace and understanding.

Our church was large and just a few could hear the man's comments to me. Many in church thought that I was wrong in stopping the woman. Nevertheless, to me it was a wrong way to show love to a fellow Christian. Rather than add guilt to his burden, I chose mercy.

 Never let your head hang down.
Never give up and sit down and grieve.
Find another way.
And don't pray when it rains if you don't pray when the sun shines.

—Satchel Paige

Reflections for Discussion

1. What is your response to "What you cannot see has to be healable"?

2. Does God have a universal plan for life?

3. "My experience neither confirms nor negates the Word of God. It stands on its own." What does this mean to you?

4. What ministries are available for disabled people in your congregation?

5. If a person is deaf or mute, is a demonic presence there?

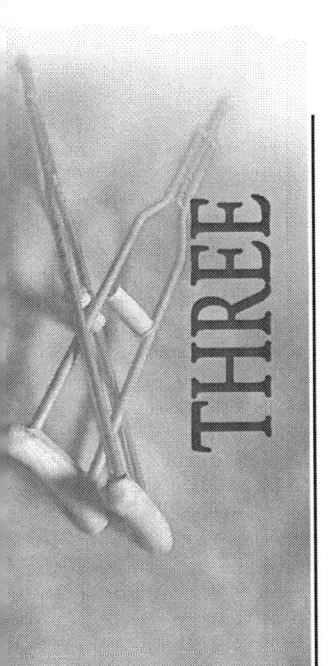

THREE

Lord, It Hurts!

"Pain is inevitable. Misery is a choice."

—Christopher Reeve

Isn't pain everywhere?

With the exception of a few forms of life, pain is universal. I have heard people moan, cry and scream from pain. I have also heard animals make heart-wrenching sounds of agonizing pain.

Where does this sting come from? Injury is most common and injury is usually a baby's first introduction to pain; that is, if a doctor did not give the baby a slap on its bottom at birth. Children will cry from hunger pangs and stomachaches as they grow. They will fall more than a hundred times before they walk. Burns from hot stoves, a sibling's swat with a toy or a bump into a table are common sources of pain.

Many years ago, I served a community ambulance company as a first aide attendant. In the early '70s, paramedics were an experiment in big cities. I went to every automobile accident, beating, burn and household calamity. With great care, those with neck and back injuries were placed on boards with neck collars. I never got over hearing their pain. Most difficult were little children injured in accidents. They were in pain and fearful of the strangers in white carrying them from their mommy, their home or car.

Can pain be measured?

Disease causes pain that is unseen to most outsiders, yet it sears the brain with fiery stabs of agony. I have heard that kidney stones and epididymitis rate as two of the most painful. I have experienced one of those mentioned, yet I believe I have encountered situations that are even more painful. Those with bone cancer, osteoporosis and rheumatoid arthritis may agree with me. Because each person has a different level of pain tolerance it is difficult to rate pain. However, when your blood pressure is through the roof, experts know how much pain you are suffering.

It is quite common to go to a pain specialist or clinic and fill out a pain questionnaire. Generally, there is a question regarding pain status on a scale of 1 to 10, with 10 as high. Staff members can chart your progress by comparing your answer with each visit. It may also be a guide to medicinal control. Another common question asks you to circle or underline descriptions of pain. Dull, aching, stabbing, shooting, constant, comes and goes, radiating, numbness and sharp are on your chart. Each person may circle one, combinations or maybe even circle them all.

Next is a "red man" chart on which clients color in red on a human body sketch from four angles. Red represents areas of pain. Again, you may color a small area, draw lines or fill in the whole drawing.

Regardless of our attempts to describe pain, it remains subjective and relative to each individual. Pain may be affected by to a person's physical position such as sitting, standing, walking or lying down. Though individuals know just how bad they feel, pain is difficult to describe succinctly. I have great regard for emergency-room personnel. While trying to understand a patient's needs, they are also comforting loved ones coming and going from waiting room to care unit. They are dealing with both physical and emotional pain.

What are some other sources of pain?

Pain from emotional loss, though often temporary, should not be off the list. Death of a loved one, loss of employment or loss of a home to fire or storm are situations we all secretly wish we will not go through. Sadly, each one of us will suffer loss of some kind during our life.

When people lose their employment, financial security is not the only thing lost. Individuals call into question their abilities and focus on failures. A middle-aged aeronautical engineer who loses his job to a lagging economy finds himself in an age-bracket that is less employable and accepts work at a department store just to pay bills. Even though the loss is genuine, I have tremendous respect for those who do not give up, but strive to retain their self-worth. Others relate this type of emotional pain to sin—a flaw in character—or to an unacceptable lifestyle. Those soothsayers, most often, have not gone through a traumatic emotional loss or have accepted a teaching that promises peace and safety by their works or service.

Two other areas of contention that are pain related are fibromyalgia and chronic fatigue syndrome. Some physicians deny the existence of fibromyalgia, while others treat it with compassion and all the skill they possess. When hearing fibromyalgia described as a mere form of depression, I ask them if they have really spoken with a person suffering horrible pain and helplessness from this disease. Adding to their pain is the usual denial of insurance benefits for patients. Chronic pain of fibromyalgia, lupus, Lyme disease, or multiple sclerosis deserves treatment as if its pain was as visible as a compound fracture.

Friends and relatives typically do not understand. After a small attempt at compassion, they tend to ignore and stay away from those suffering. Spouses of fibromyalgia patients experience frustrations when their loved ones are passed around by the medical profession and are shunned by friends and relatives.

Chronic fatigue syndrome is another condition that deserves mentioning because the symptoms are similar to those associated with influenza (muscle aches, headache and fatigue). Unlike influenza, CFS symptoms may ebb and flow, but they never go away. (Imagine dealing with flu symptoms on a daily basis and you know how someone with CFS feels on a good day.)

Primary symptoms of CFS include a new onset of fatigue or tiredness that lasts for at least six months and is not relieved by normal rest. It is a full-body fatigue, serious enough to restrict normal activity. It develops from far less exertion than was possible before the illness. Other symptoms include constant headaches that may differ in pattern and severity, feeling tired after a normal time of sleep, forgetfulness, confusion or difficulty in concentrating, and irritability. In addition, there may be joint pain, low-grade fever (101° F or less), lymph node tenderness and swelling in the neck or armpit. Muscle aches, muscle fatigue that lasts more than 24 hours after a normally tolerated exercise, unexplained muscle weakness and a red, sore throat are also symptomatic.

Often Chronic Fatigue Syndrome and chronic fatigue are mistaken as being synonymous. Chronic fatigue is often a symptom of other conditions such as depression, sleep apnea or a common sickness. Patients can get relief as specific symptoms, which cause it, are treated.

At this writing, there is no cure or complete relief for Chronic Fatigue Syndrome.

Do I deserve this?

I have not listed all sources of pain. It would take scientific journals, texts and a team of research assistants to list them all. Still someone may ask, "What did I do to deserve this?" This life of pain is not what I expected. "Why me, when those around me live a life of health and joyfulness?" I do know that a new study has shown that those with chronic back pain who have forgiven others, experience lower levels of pain and less associated psychological problems, such as anger and depression, than those who have not forgiven.

If this sounds too simplistic, it will not cost to try it. As I have mentioned, there is physical pain and emotional pain. They typically coexist in people. Walking in faith means that you are following our Lord's teachings to forgive others as we ask them to forgive us. In the Lord's Prayer, He said, "And forgive us our debts, as we also have forgiven (left, remitted, and let go of the debts, and have given up resentment against) our debtors" (Matthew 6:12, *Amp.*).

This is more difficult than most people realize. You are asking God to forgive you precisely as you have forgiven an unfaithful spouse, a perpetrator of a crime against you or your family, or a broken family relationship.

> *Resentment is like taking poison and hoping the other person dies.*
>
> —St. Augustine

Forgiveness is difficult because you must give up something. As an example, to forgive an unfaithful spouse, you must give up that grudge or feeling that justifies the anger and resentment.

I mentioned this to a singles group one evening and questions started flying. "You mean I must forgive what he or she did to me?" My answer was, "Yes, but I do not expect you to forget it." Forgiveness is a real act of faith, while forgetting is an act of the mind. Most healthy minds remember unfair and painful life situations. A major difference is that when you truly forgive, you covenant with yourself, "I will never mention this matter again." This is similar to God's forgiveness of your sins. He will never throw them in your face again. They are in "His sea of forgetfulness."

We need to create our own lake of forgetfulness and make it so deep that is it is very difficult to mention. Love is the water in your lake covering a hurt. Will all of your physical pain leave? I cannot say, but if you practice forgiveness, you will live with your pain and be more lovable to live with.

How can I get relief from this pain?

Prayer takes a back seat when it should be a first-action response to pain. Typically, individuals go to their medicine chest for an analgesic to relieve pain first. When pain fails to subside, they call a doctor and if relief does not come, prayer comes to mind. Preferably, prayer should begin at the onset of pain and accompany individuals during recovery.

> This *is* my comfort in my affliction: for thy word hath quickened me (Psalm 119:50, KJV).

A genuine confidence in the Word does bring comfort. I have always found relief while listening to my favorite type of Christian music. Music does make a heart merry, and it is difficult for pain to gain much control when someone is full of joy. Hymns, songs and choruses are filled with Scripture and words of hope. Hope must not be lost because it is an important portion of faith. It is the faith that tells a weightlifter he can lift immense iron weights. Faith perceives a reality that the senses cannot. It is hope that gives the mind strength to accept what the spirit knows as fact.

Do doctors and medicine help relieve pain?

Yes, doctors and medicine may relieve or control pain. I am personally thankful to be living in a time of medical breakthroughs. As a young boy, living with my parents in what was then French Morocco, my best friend and another playmate contracted polio. I had been staying in the home of my playmate while my Naval aviator father was gone and my mother was on a trip with other Navy wives. The evening of the diagnosis, my father flew in to get the other children and took me to our base dispensary. I received two shots of gamma-globulin, as Salk vaccine was not yet available. I was spared from polio, yet my friends lost the use of their legs. Today, polio is considered a conquered disease, as is smallpox.

I am so thankful to the Lord for giving us men and women who study and work hard to become physicians that bring healing to the sick and comfort to those who are dying. Many people are afraid that drug addiction will become a problem while controlling pain. As long as the doctor's directions are followed, it should not be a concern. Everyone reacts to medication in different ways, so it is of vital importance not to take someone else's medication. You may have a well-meaning friend who wishes to save you money. However, wisdom dictates that your medicine should come from your doctor.

Medicine is expensive, but a person can take advantage of insurance, a new Medicare Drug program and free medicine, which is available with prescription from drug companies. Following are two free programs found during a Google® Web search: *www.freemedicineprogram.com* and *www.freemedicinefoundation.com*.

Does exercise help?

After surgery, it is common for doctors to recommend walking as exercise. This is not just a vain statement. It is a fact that proper exercise will aid in recovery and reduction of pain. Exercise should be gentle at first and under the guidance of a physical therapist. Gentle exercise, beginning with strength building as a finish to therapy, is a practical recovery program.

All too often, people decide on their own exercise program and cause more injury rather than healing. They will push until pain increases, basing their exercise program on, "no pain, no gain." Pain is a signal that something is wrong. It is what sent you to the hospital. Why damage that which surgery repaired? Patients need to remember the term *patient* or *patience*. Once again, we are faced with, "I need it now, and I want it now."

What about depression?

I often think of my ancestors who lived good lives without our medical and medicinal miracles of today. They lived with pain and acceptance. I had a great uncle who, as a young boy, sliced his knee joint with a scythe. He cut his main tendons and did not have an orthopedic surgeon to repair the damage. For the remainder of his life he had to wear a heavy metal brace, stiffly attached to his upper leg. He was crippled, though I never heard him complain. I was amazed to watch him repair shoes with skills like a modern machine. He never had a government rehabilitation program, food stamps or physical therapy. He did have a family and a strong will to be productive. The world owed him nothing. His words were always kind because he loved the Lord and His Word.

Did my uncle go through depression after his accident, knowing of the crippled lifestyle ahead? I do not know, but I can reasonably say, "Yes, he did, but he recovered." Pain causes depression, and depression increases pain. My uncle did not have the luxury of antidepressants as we have today, but he found a way out. I am thankful for medication to deal with depression; it is just amazing how our grandparents and great-grandparents lived without them.

Depression should receive treatment along with pain. After the Vietnam War, at a Chicago veterans' hospital, patients with chronic pain found relief when given antidepressants as part of their pain regimen. Today it is common for a patient with chronic pain to be treated by a psychiatrist, along with a pain specialist. Both work well together to speed recovery or aid in an improved lifestyle.

There is no disgrace in going to a psychiatrist. That fear is outdated. I encourage those with chronic pain to seek a psychiatrist who will meet personal physical, mental and, significantly, spiritual needs.

One big problem with depression is that we do not feel like doing the things that will make us better. Getting outdoors and walking just a little each day will help relieve the barrier of fear and misguided attitude. You think, *I will get out tomorrow*, yet tomorrow never comes until there is a change in attitude. Getting out and moving about will become natural once again. You will start to feel normal again—and normal is a wonderful feeling when you have been depressed.

We go to great lengths to find relief, because pain is expensive. It takes away from on-the-job time, and costs great amounts of personal money. Approximately 75 million Americans are uninsured or underinsured. Even symptomatic treatment with medication is expensive, not to mention a surgical solution.

When my daughter was in high school, she had a cactus spine embedded in her heel. I could not see any visible sign of it, yet every step she took caused pain. Although the doctor could not visibly identify her source of pain, he did believe her. With a quick move of his scalpel, her pain was relieved. So was I.

The reason I mention that cactus spine is to point out that no matter how severe its cause, people want relief as soon as possible, even if the source of pain is not obvious. Hip, knee and back surgeries number in the thousands as individuals seek help from their suffering. They may have repeated surgeries and still have pain as a constant companion for years. I personally have had 15 major spinal surgeries, with additional related surgeries. I live with pain every moment of my day. I am now facing another major spinal surgery. Each one has been necessary, although some operations have been a result of failed previous procedures or ongoing disease.

How much pain must I endure before I can find relief?

This is a difficult question. I remember a painful two-hour surgical procedure in which I was awake. I asked the Lord to help me and to end my pain. He did not answer immediately. As I was wheeled from an operating room, my anesthetist assistant was shaking a bag of narcotic syringes. His comment was, "I have never given anyone this amount of pain med and they stayed awake." It was not until I got into a hospital bed and could change positions that my pain subsided.

Where was the Lord? He was with me all the time.

> But He said to me, My grace (My favor and lovingkindness and mercy) is enough for you [sufficient against any danger and enables you to bear the trouble manfully]; for *My* strength *and* power are made perfect (fulfilled and completed) *and show themselves most effective* in [your] weakness. Therefore, I will all the more gladly glory in my weaknesses *and* infirmities, that the strength *and* power of Christ (the Messiah) may rest (yes, may pitch a tent over and dwell) upon me! (2 Corinthians 12:9, *Amp.*).

Think about this: God's one and only Son, Jesus Christ (the one perfect man to ever step foot on earth) was abandoned to die on the cross. With nails driven through His hands and feet, He was stripped, spit upon, beaten and mocked. As He hung on the cross, He bore the sins of the entire world. Christ cried out, "My God, My God, why have You forsaken Me?" (Matthew 27:46). In order for God to save you and me, He offered His Son as a sacrifice for our sins.

He suffered physical pain and emotional pain as He accepted God's will. I am always cognizant that I must be thankful for a God who loved me so much, that in spite of my failures, He gave His Son to die for me. How can I complain about my pain when Jesus suffered even more just for me? Then I am always reminded that there are other people who suffer more than I do, and I tell myself how fortunate I really am. Christ died for them as well.

Reflections for Discussion

1. What did Christopher Reeve mean by "Pain is inevitable, misery is a choice?"

2. How do you describe pain so that another person will understand its level of severity?

3. What losses have occurred in your life, and how did they affect your lifestyle?

4. Forgiveness is mentioned as difficult because you must give something up. What do you have to give up to forgive the person who has caused you pain and loss?

5. How much pain must I endure before I find relief? Share your feelings.

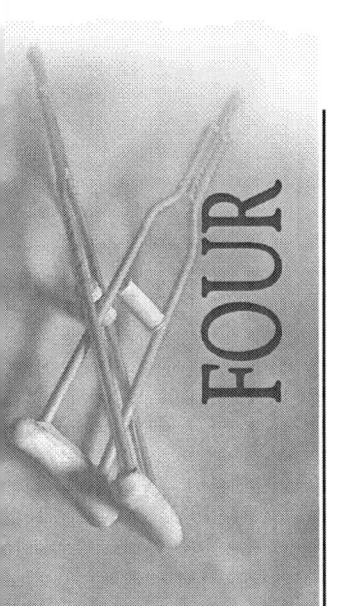

FOUR

Is Something Wrong With My Faith?

What is God saying to me today?

To understand the basics of our faith, we must accept God's Word as a love letter to us. Read His letter in a way that allows you to receive every nuance. The importance of understanding God's Word is emphasized by this scripture: "But Jesus replied to them, You are wrong because you know neither the Scriptures nor God's power" (Matthew 22:29, Amp.).

> ❝ Faith is believing what you do not see; the reward of faith is to see what you believe. ❞
> —St. Augustine

A Catholic nun in our city was known as a great person of prayer, and she had great faith in the power of prayer. She would pray for hours on

"He who loses money, loses much; He who loses a friend, loses much more, He who loses faith, loses all."

—Eleanor Roosevelt

end. Once when asked how she knew when to stop praying, she replied, "My knower goes off." She had faith that God would let her know when her prayer time was sufficient. Her faith did not depend upon something she could see, touch, hear or smell. Rather, it had an intuitive effect on her spirit.

Belief in, devotion to, or trust in somebody or something, especially without logical proof, is a description of faith. This statement *without logical proof* is a general hang up for most people. Yet, we accept theory when its partial meaning is a set of statements or principles devised to explain a group of facts that can be proven or explained by natural phenomena. Once again, we deal with another questionable term—phenomenon, which means "an unusual, significant, or unaccountable fact or occurrence; a marvel." [1]

Science depends upon theory and theorems, just as a believer depends upon faith. If our logical mind can believe in an unaccountable fact or occurrence (a marvel), then what is our difficulty with faith that believes in, is devoted to or trusts in somebody or something without proof? A bonus for faith is the historical fact that Jesus was born of a Virgin, crucified for our sins, resurrected from the dead and now sits at the right hand of God.

The long and winding road of life takes us through regions of pain, doubts, questions and suffering. Can your faith stand the strain of a long and winding journey? How can we make it home?

It seems hard to understand.

Even with definitions and attempts of allegory, many

people still have difficulty understanding and explaining faith. A predominate aspect of faith is that it does not demand proof.

When my father was alive, while we were having lunch together, he questioned my faith. He said my faith is based on meekness, which automatically disqualified it. Referring to Eastern belief, he commented that he could prove to me that the table at which we were sitting did not exist. His statements were so off-the-wall that, out of respect, I remained silent. I thought to myself that I could prove that the table did exist by dropping it on his foot! His resulting pain would be proof that something of substantial substance had hit him.

I also mused that if he thought meekness was a weakness, then Mahatma Gandhi, whom my father respected, changed the nation of India with a secret potion rather than passive resistance. I refrained from an argument, because it would have solved nothing at that time. Also, it might have prevented any future chances for me to witness to him.

Your faith will be challenged by your relatives, friends, coworkers and other non-believers. You might question your own faith during a severe illness, injury or tragedy. Nevertheless, most Christians will return quickly to their faith through the aid of a pastor, Christian counselor or in their own private meditations. Even though faith is difficult to understand, it is very difficult to lose without a volitional dismissal.

The extreme simplicity of faith is nothing more than believing God will do what He says He will do. Our part is to trust Him to do it. We have all trusted others to do things for us because of the confidence we had in them. You may have hired a carpenter to build a house or a plumber to fix a drain. If any one asks me what it means to trust someone else to work for me, I answer that it means just letting them do it, and not feeling it necessary to do it myself. We often put our trust in people we barely know.

Why do others question our faith?

To say that you or I must have something wrong with our faith often comes from a teaching, book or sermon on faith that another has accepted as doctrine. This could subject you to a guilt trip because you think you have displeased God. That's when we remember these words:

"For I am persuaded, that neither death, nor life, nor angels, nor principalities, nor powers, nor things present, nor things to come, nor height, nor depth, nor any other creature, shall be able to separate us from the love of God, which is in Christ Jesus our Lord" (Romans 8:38, 39, KJV).

This scripture from Romans gives us confidence in a heavenly Father who will never walk out the door and desert us in time of need. This scripture should solidify faith in times of difficulty and remind us of the sureties of God's love and presence. Jesus knew pain and suffering long before we existed. He will never reject our call for help. "He will not fail you" (Deuteronomy 4:31, *Amp.*) or leave you. "I am with you always," Christ says in Matthew 28:20, "even to the end of the age." Loneliness and rejection are temporary when we place our trust in Christ and realize that He will deliver from isolation.

Isaiah tells us that Christ was "despised and forsaken of men, a man of sorrows and acquainted with grief" (Isaiah 53:3, *NASB*). While we have little knowledge of Jesus' early years, imagine the pressure, rejection and loneliness Jesus must have experienced as a perfect, sinless child in a world full of evil. It was not until His resurrection that His own family members realized who He really was. His mother always knew.

My friend once mentioned in a sermon called, "Why I Believe in the Virgin Birth," that Mary herself is proof of the virgin birth. What mother would allow her son to suffer the torture, beatings and horrific death on the cross if it were not true? She could have very easily said that it was all a lie, and her Son would have been set free. Mary could not do that because she knew the truth. She knew who Jesus was and had faith that if He died, He would rise again. Her faith kept her on solid ground throughout His life and death. We do see a mother's concern when Jesus was 12 and appeared lost from the family on the trip home. To me, that is just a good mother. As you know, Jesus was about His Father's business, teaching in the synagogue.

When an individual's faith is unwavering, it is often referred to as "Pit Bull" faith. Pit Bulls make good guard dogs because when they bite, their jaws lock tight. The dog will not let go until he is disabled or its victim is subdued. That is the faith I personally desire. I will never let go of God until evil is subdued or I am healed. It is that kind of faith that has taken me this far.

❝ *I know God will not give me anything I can't handle. I just wish He wouldn't trust me so much.* ❞

—Mother Teresa

Why are others healed?

Is there something wrong with my faith when Jack is healed and I am not? Just because I am not healed does not mean God is out of the healing business. I have close friends who do not believe in taking pills for relief and depend upon God for their healing. However, they have incurred diseases that required medical intervention. These situations are repeated the world over. Somewhere a person receives a miraculous healing from a deadly disease, whereas another continues in pain and suffering. Does this mean that God is inconsistent? Absolutely not, Scripture tells us that the Lord is the same today, yesterday and tomorrow (Hebrews 13:8).

So then, what is the difference? Let me give a couple of examples of our own inconsistencies. While sharing a meal with an evangelist who had just spoken at our church, I noticed an inconsistency in his observations on healing. During his sermon, he stated that he had never been to a doctor in his life. This was amazing, as I would have estimated his age as late 60s. As he was eating, I noticed that his teeth were full of fillings. Had he mislead our church? No, he just did not equate tooth decay and dentists with disease and doctors. Tooth decay is a form of disease. It is the formation of cavities in the teeth by bacteria. If untreated, it can lead to the death of the tooth. The common solution is a visit to the family dentist and by the way, a dentist is a doctor.

My next example is our acceptance of a common cold and rejection of cancer. Very few people seek out their pastor or doctor when they have a cold. They may take over-the-counter decongestants and cough syrups, and let it take its course. If these individuals had been told after a yearly physical that there is a spot on their lungs, they would immediately fear cancer. Before their tests to confirm a benign or malignant tumor, they would have told relatives, friends and pastors to pray for a negative report on their test. If their test is positive, great amounts of prayer will go before our Lord for healing.

I believe you can see my point. God is not inconsistent, we are. In a subconscious manner, we have established a rating system for sickness, when in reality, there is none. Disease is an impairment of the normal state of the human body, or one of its parts, that interrupts or modifies the performance of its vital functions. It is a response to environmental factors (malnutrition, industrial hazards, or climate), to specific infective agents (worms, bacteria, or viruses), to inherent defects of the organism (as genetic anomalies), or to combinations of these factors.[2]

I am grateful that God has given us medicine and doctors, along with breakthrough research that occurs. In recent news, a young Australian boy had both hands and a foot severed in an unusual basketball accident. If you were his parent, would you leave him where he fell and just pray while precious blood and time are being lost? I doubt it. Doctors were able to reattach all three limbs, and life had returned to the boy's hands and foot. Nerve response will take time to develop. As good parents, they sought medical help, and I feel safe in saying they prayed for the healing of their son. There was no lack of faith in the parents, just good judgment and an access to excellent medical facilities.

> Looking unto Jesus the author and finisher of *our* faith; who for the joy that was set before him endured the cross, despising the shame, and is set down at the right hand of the throne of God (Hebrews 12:2, KJV).

Many have asked me for the meaning of this Scripture. The word *author* means "a chief leader—author, captain, prince." The meaning of *finisher* is "(the state) *completeness* (mental or moral)—perfection (-ness)." By putting both meanings together, we might say that Jesus is our leader who has given us completeness and perfection. He is the Creator of our faith, and it is perfect. Faith is not something that contains variables—it is perfect, just as the author of it is perfect.

Our human frailty leads us to doubt our faith, its strength and reality. Scripture tells us, "Without faith, it is impossible to please him," (Hebrews 11:6, KJV). In many years past, this scripture was used to humble church members. I remember running to the altar to pray and seek His forgiveness every Sunday, as if I had lost something during the week. The truth is that faith is something God gives us, and He does not take it away frivolously.

How can I say that I do not have enough faith if God has given it to me? Depending upon denominational beliefs, some will say that faith is a spiritual gift to be used at special times when the Holy Spirit directs the individual. Others will say God gives us all a measure of faith that is equal among all believers. Arguments abound in regard to this question, and all arguments create is anger. I prefer a mix of both, realizing that God has given me a measure of faith. Under extraordinary circumstances, my faith may lead to a miraculous event.

Faith is only as good as the object of that faith. "I'll go down if father will hold the rope," was the offer of a Highland lad, when a traveler wanted him to reach the eggs of a wild bird that had built its nest on a rocky ledge. The boy felt that there would be no danger if the rope was in his father's hand, because he had a powerful arm, a loving heart and would not allow his own child to perish.

> ❝ What seem our worst prayers may really be, in God's eyes, our best. Those, I mean, which are least supported by devotional feeling. For these may come from a deeper level than feeling. God sometimes seems to speak to us most intimately when he catches us, as it were, off our guard. ❞
>
> —C.S. Lewis

Are there signs of a lack of faith?

A sign of our lack of faith in His love may be how we respond to trials. If we believe in how much He loves us and we have read and heard the extent of that love, then we know our trial is for our good. Because of His love, we should know that a trial is not just an arbitrary act without reason. Because He is God, trials cannot be occurring without His awareness or concern. It definitely is not an act just to make our lives more difficult. A child may think this way while receiving a spanking, but we should not.

Another way to measure the strength of our faith is to list things we think would make our lives better, yet seem out of reach. For some, it is health, money, a job; and still others, a mate. If our list seems greater than God, then some self-examination is needed. When we place greater importance on things rather than His love, we are straying from His good will for us. God tells us, "For the Lord God is a sun and shield: the Lord will give grace and glory: no good thing will he withhold from them that walk uprightly" (Psalm 84:11, KJV).

As children, our parents disciplined us. While being punished, how often did we thank them for the love they were showing us? As parents, you have disciplined your children. How many times have they ever said, "Thank you"? Most likely, your answer to both is "Never!" Yet, it is during these times of trial or discipline that God is close to us. If we would divert our attention from our problems and think more of others, then we would become emissaries of His love.

As Jesus reaches out to us when we are in need, He also wants us to reach out to others. Think of coworkers or acquaintances that seem lonely or depressed. What can you do to make them feel appreciated? Sometimes all it takes is a smile or a few encouraging words to brighten someone's day.

Whenever you feel helpless and isolated from friends or family, remember that Christ offered His life for you. You are worth more to Jesus than you can ever imagine. His Word is there to reassure you—but only if you read it consistently.

We must be reminded that there is an undeviating connection between faith and the Word. God could not separate one from the other any more than we could separate the rays from the sun. God's Word is the foundation whereby faith is supported and constant. If faith turns away from the Word, it fails and if the Word is taken away, no faith will then remain.

John's Gospel tells us, "These things have been written that you may believe" (see John 20:31). Paul tells us "faith comes from hearing the message, and the message is heard through the word of Christ" (Romans 10:17, *NIV*). If someone should ask, "How can I increase my faith?" the answer is to saturate your mind with God's Word.

> *I believe the Bible is the best gift God has ever given to men. All the good from the Savior of the world is communicated to us through this book.*
>
> —Abraham Lincoln (1809-1865)

Endnotes

[1] (*Phenomenon* as defined by) *The American Heritage® Dictionary of the English Language*, Fourth Edition Copyright © 2000 by Houghton Mifflin Company.

[2] (*Disease* as defined by) *Merriam-Webster Medical Dictionary*, © 2002 Merriam-Webster, Inc.

Reflections for Discussion

1. Describe the meaning of faith without the use of logical proof.

2. Have you ever felt that there was something wrong with your or another's faith? If you have, what was the occasion?

3. What does the author mean when he states that we have a "rating system" for sickness?

4. How can a person say that they do not have enough faith, if God has given it to them?

5. Does faith have levels of measurement?

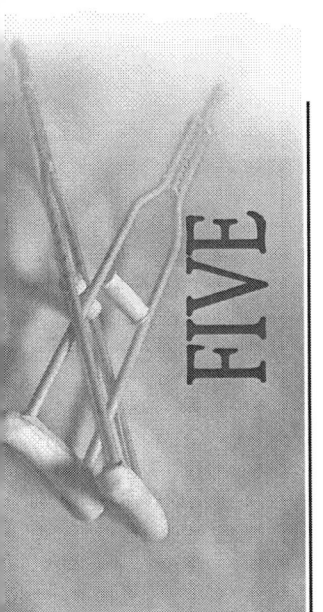

FIVE

How Long Will It Last?

When will the pain stop?

When trials and calamities overcome us, we are resentful or overcome with grief. However, trials and calamities are blessings to the believer. They are unforeseen opportunities. Look to Jesus. If He had not been crucified, He may have died an old prophet, and history would have forgotten Him. History better records His resurrection than it does Napoleon's defeat at Waterloo. Because He was crucified and resurrected, you and I have a stable foundation of faith based on facts rather than myths or legends.

We have heard of beatings by the Jews in the Sanhedrin and scourging by the Romans. The crown of thorns, the heavy beam, the climb to Golgotha

> *"Sometimes God has to put us flat on our back before we are looking up to Him."*
>
> —Jack Graham

and the agony of the cross have been described, but have you considered the nails? According to doctors, piercing of the median nerve of the hands with a nail can cause pain so immense that even morphine will not help. The excruciating pain runs like a lightning bolt up the arm and into the spine. Driving a nail through the foot's plantar nerve would have a similar effect of suffering. However, we must remember that Scripture says, "But He *was* wounded for our transgressions, *He was* bruised for our iniquities; the chastisement for our peace *was* upon Him, and by His stripes we are healed" (Isaiah 53:5).

Am I happy when my life is full of pain? Yes, not for pain, but for opportunities that arise to minister to others. I do not give them sympathy, for that is just an "I hope you get well." Rather, I have empathy, an ability to feel and relate to others. Empathy is an action rather than an emotion. I never say, "I know how you feel." Instead my reply to others is, "I believe that I can feel and relate to your situation."

Now your big question is, "How long must I suffer? When will the pain stop?" I have always tried to understand the apostle Paul and his thorn in his flesh. "And lest I should be exalted above measure through the abundance of the revelations, there was given to me a thorn in the flesh, the messenger of Satan to buffet me, lest I should be exalted above measure" (2 Corinthians 12:7, KJV).

I have heard and read many interpretations of Paul's affliction ranging from a demonic attack to his mother-in-law. I previously mentioned that I like to be pragmatic, and perhaps you will consider this scenario. "And there came thither *certain* Jews from Antioch and Iconium, who persuaded the people, and, having stoned Paul, drew *him* out of the city, supposing he had been dead" (Acts 14:19, KJV).

Paul was stoned to a point of perceived death. Stoning was a brutal form of execution. Generally, the person to be stoned was bound, hands and feet, and pushed into a pit commonly used for this vicious act. The action of falling 10 feet alone would cause massive contusions and possible broken bones. The stones were not marble sized, but baseball to softball size or larger. If stoning failed to kill its victim, he would be run through with swords. Consider this picture now, Paul was thrown into a pit and a group of men threw stones continually on him until they thought he was dead. Then they dragged him out of the city to a place for the dead.

"However, when the disciples gathered around him, he rose up and went into the city. And the next day he departed with Barnabas to Derbe" (Acts 14:20).

The preceding Scripture leaves little room for misinterpretation. Disciples gathered around him, and he came to life. The next day he began a journey. What we do not know is if Paul was healed of all his injuries from his stoning. I would assume that he had received a concussion, massive contusions and broken bones. I agree that he miraculously lived, although there is no direct statement of complete physical healing. Many have assumed as much from the fact that he rose up. I wonder who set his broken bones and healed his concussion? If God, then what a blessed event! If he healed naturally over time, he may have suffered in his older age of migraines, arthritis or other ailments from the stoning.

As I mentioned before, I am a pragmatic person, and I believe that his thorn in the flesh may have been some lingering effect of his stoning. *Strong's Concordance* describes thorn as "(figurative a bodily *annoyance* or *disability*)."

"And lest I should be exalted above measure through the abundance of the revelations, there was given to me a thorn in the flesh, the messenger of Satan to buffet me, lest I should be exalted above measure" (2 Corinthians 12:7, KJV).

Paul did not live a life free of pain and calamities; however, he used them to his advantage in ministry. God's minister is not required be a picture of health who drinks carrot juice for breakfast and runs two miles each day. His ministers need to be humble and compassionate. That, I believe, is what Paul meant when he said that he was reminded of his human disabilities so that he would not consider himself above a common person.

Speaking of Paul: "His letters are brawny and potent, but in person he's a weakling and mumbles when he talks" (2 Corinthians 10:10, *TM*).

Were there others besides Paul?

I am certain that Bible characters such as Job and Jeremiah often wondered if God had "plugged His ears" to their cries of pain. Job was separated from people other than his friends, and Jeremiah was cast into a dungeon, or a pit full of mire.

What had each one done wrong? As for Job, he got Satan's attention, and Jeremiah angered his king's princes by foretelling the truth. They had done nothing wrong as such, but, for God's glory, they were allowed to suffer. Their suffering and deliverance has been a source of encouragement for millions.

Many have debated what Job must have felt. Though Job suffered, he never gave up on God. "For I know *that* my Redeemer lives, and He shall stand at last on the earth; and after my skin is destroyed, this *I know,* that in my flesh I shall see God" (Job 19:25, 26).

No matter what you feel or what happens, God does exist and He loves you deeply. No matter how awful things become, no matter what happens, we will never be separated from God's love.

Jeremiah was thrown into a pit of mire for doing the Lord's work. Did he question "Why?" or "When will I get out of this muck?" He did not question "why?," but he may have wondered *how long is this misery of being stuck in mud without water to drink going to last?*

"Then took they Jeremiah, and cast him into the dungeon of Malchiah the son of Hammelech, that *was* in the court of the prison: and they let down Jeremiah with cords. And in the dungeon *there was* no water, but mire: so Jeremiah sunk in the mire" (Jeremiah 38:6, KJV).

Jeremiah was fortunate to have a friend in court who procured his release. The pit must have been deep and the mud like a form of quicksand, because it took 30 men to pull him up from the mire. I do not know of a modern-day person who would enjoy that experience. They would ask either *why* or *when* will this end?

Will it go away?

Many have had accidents, therefore explaining the "why." Their recovery process will cause some to ask how long. Others ask, "How long will I live?" after receiving a poor prognosis. We want either our pain to leave speedily or life to be extended indefinitely. The following Scripture should speak loudly to you when asking why or how long.

> Keep a cool head. Stay alert. The Devil is poised to pounce, and would like nothing better than to catch you napping. Keep your guard up. You're not the only ones plunged into these hard times. It's the same with Christians all over the world. So keep a firm grip on the faith. The suffering won't last forever. It won't be long before this generous God who has great plans for us in Christ—eternal and glorious plans they are!—will have you put together and on your feet for good. He gets the last word; yes, he does (1 Peter 5:8-11, *TM*).

For a majority of people, their pain will go away following an injury, accident, surgery or illness. Natural healing will be their main source of relief from suffering and pain. Our body is wonderfully made, and within it is the amazing ability to heal itself. A simple hang nail causes pain, but when it is removed, it heals. Small children often get their fingers slammed in a car door, but they heal naturally without a doctor or a splint. Consider our ancestors who were without modern medicine. They healed of wounds, injuries and ills that would cause people today to seek medical aid for a cure.

Like me, many people depend on medicine to control their pain. I have an intrathecal drug pump and an implanted tens unit. This pump places pain medication directly to my spine without any effort on my part. The tens unit in my lower back sends small electrical surges in varying patterns and intensity down my back and legs to cover pain from damaged nerves. Without these devices, I would be a complete invalid, unable to walk, drive or have a meaningful quality of life. I would be taking oral medication that has dangerous side effects and is potentially habit-forming.

There are others suffering with pain of cancer, lupus, Lyme disease or multiple sclerosis who use these drug pumps. Tens units have been in use for quite a few years as an external unit, but more recently they are implanted. The use of chemotherapy, radiation therapy and cancer-suppressing drugs are improving and prolonging the lives of many. Cancer is no longer a definite death warrant. Children with spinal scoliosis can be corrected with surgery and lead a normal life. No longer does a clubfoot mean a life with a limp or an altered walk. These examples are just the tip of the needle of medical solutions for which our society is grateful.

Then there is the miraculous healing that a dear soul receives in prayer, worship or devotion. We all desire the miraculous, while others spurn and criticize those who believe and preach healing through the Holy Spirit as a gift of God. Perhaps one of the most famous proponents of God's healing in the 20th century was Oral Roberts. There are documented healings, confirmed by physicians because of his ministry. However, many went forward for prayer and did not walk away healed.

The miraculous will always leave us with the question of why did God choose to heal that person and not another. I do not have that answer, although I received a miraculous healing from glaucoma while I continue to live each day in pain. Why He chose to heal my eyes and not my spine I will never know, but it will never change my walk with Him.

For some, pain and suffering may last a short time and then return. They may have mild symptoms that, with a small diet or schedule adjustment, will allow them to lead a somewhat normal life. Others must make major changes, giving up their favorite activities or work style in order to live with their condition. Tragically, others become so ill that they are unable to work and struggle daily to meet life's needs. For some, pain may last a lifetime.

What about chronic illness?

A chronic condition is a birth defect, disease, disorder or injury that a person has to live with continually. Chronic illnesses are marked by a long duration or frequent recurrence over a long time and often with a slow progressing severity. The condition lasts a year or longer, limits activity and may require ongoing care. More than 90 million Americans live with chronic illnesses. Chronic diseases account for 70 percent of all deaths in the United States.

For many, an illness will go undiagnosed for several years. Thousands of people become depressed and overwhelmed, without answers as to why their bodies will not function normally. When they do receive a diagnosis, it may take months or even years to regulate medications. Even still, they live with constant tests to adjust their medication and manage the side effects. Although they try multiple therapies, physicians and medications, unfortunately there is little or no relief.

Consider the following illustration when asking "Why me?" and "How long?"

> The only survivor of a shipwreck washed up on a small, uninhabited island. He prayed relentlessly for God to rescue him and every day he scanned the horizon for help, but none seemed forthcoming. Exhausted, he eventually managed to build a little hut out of driftwood to protect him from the elements and to store his few possessions. Then one day, after scavenging for food, he arrived home to find his little hut in flames, the smoke rolling up to the sky. The worst had happened—everything was lost. He was stunned with grief and anger. "God, how could You do this to me?" he cried.
>
> Early the next day, he awoke to the sound of a ship that was approaching the island. It had come to rescue him. "How did you know I was here?" the weary man asked his rescuers. "We saw your smoke signal," they replied.
>
> It is easy to become discouraged when things are going bad. However, we should not lose hope; God is at work in our lives, even in the midst of pain and suffering. Remember, next time your little hut is burning to the ground, it just may be a smoke signal that summons God's grace"
>
> —Author unknown

"And we know that all things work together for good to those who love God, to those who are the called according to His purpose" (Romans 8:28).

How should we respond to ongoing pain?

When in private discussion with unbelievers or a marginal Christian, I am ultimately asked this question: "How can a loving God allow suffering, war, disease and famine, especially to the seemingly innocent?"

The "problem of pain," as C.S. Lewis noted, "is that it is atheism's most potent weapon against the Christian faith." Our world is now under God's Curse (Genesis 3:17) because of man's rebellion against God's Word. This corruption mentioned in Romans 8:21 and 22 coexists with our world groaning as in labor pains that affects all of mankind universally. God did not create our world like this and He will change it back. His Word gives this wonderful promise:

> And God will wipe away every tear from their eyes; there shall be no more death, nor sorrow, nor crying. There shall be no more pain, for the former things have passed away (Revelation 21:4).

Along this path of long-term pain and suffering, we have two choices: become angry with God and others or become closer to our heavenly Father.

Anger is a common choice to a tragedy, but most people work through it and move on to acceptance. If they choose to remain angry, then their life exudes bitterness, sullen withdrawal, despair and depression. Others find their situation to be very uncomfortable and begin to avoid the angry person, which merely adds to his or her loneliness and depression.

I remember visiting a person years ago who had difficulty following a spinal surgery. Several screws holding the hardware had become loose, causing pain. I never heard a word of kindness or compassion from that person, even after multiple visits. His anger was directed at his spouse, family members, doctors and God. Sadly, his spouse developed cancer and passed away. All alone, the angry person disappeared into the streets of the city.

My grandfather chose the second option—to become closer to God—as did another wonderful person I knew. Both continued their lay ministry by having home meetings during the week. They exuded kindness and love to everyone around them—especially those who aided them. In spite of pain and knowledge that death was not far off, they continued to keep their families and others warm with thanksgiving and kind words.

It was always a pleasure to be around them, and I always left feeling more blessed than blessing. As you may have surmised, both were devoted Christians, each from a different denomination but serving their Savior. From the home ministry of one, a strong church was born that continues to grow and minister to its community.

> *The highest honor that God can confer upon his children is the blood-red crown of martyrdom. The jewels of a Christian are his afflictions. The regalia of the kings that God has made are their troubles, their sorrows, and their griefs. Griefs exalt us, and troubles lift us.*
>
> —Charles Spurgeon

Reflections for Discussion

1. Does the author's analysis of Paul's stoning and recovery have validity, or do you feel that the "thorn" was from another source?

2. Does the miraculous leave us with the question of why God choose to heal one person and not another?

3. The "problem of pain," as C.S. Lewis noted, "is that it is atheism's most potent weapon against the Christian faith." How do you reply to the question of pain and suffering?

4. Have you ever been angry with God? Why or why not?

5. Do you agree with this statement by Charles Spurgeons, "Griefs exalt us, and troubles lift us?"

SIX

Why Am I So Depressed?

"If we were never depressed we would not be alive—only material things don't suffer depression. If human beings were not capable of depression, we would have no capacity for happiness and exaltation. Whenever you examine yourself, take into account your capacity for depression"

—Oswald Chambers
My Utmost for His Highest

Is depression a natural reaction?

This chapter is not intended to be a medical dissertation on depression. If the following assists in your understanding of depression or leads you to seek treatment, then it will have accomplished its purpose.

Yes, it is part of your emotional make up with which God created us. Perhaps you can remember as a child when a favorite pet died of old age or was killed by an automobile. You probably cried and asked your parents why Spot died. Then you spent a few days in mourning. You may not have recognized it as mourning. You felt down in the dumps, which, as adults, we recognize as depression. However, after a few days you were your normal self. Perhaps your parents took you to a pet store or the local animal shelter to find a new pet. Spot was replaced with a vibrant puppy and soon was only a pleasant memory. You no longer mourned or felt sadness with each thought of the loss of your pet.

As I have said before, pain and depression are often related when pain is chronic. I only repeat this to reaffirm that you are not mentally diseased if you experience depression while living with long-term pain and suffering. It is very common for open-heart surgery patients to become depressed during recovery, though it often leaves as quickly as it arrived.

One statistic states that one in five people will go through a serious depression in their lifetime. Generally, it is only those who attempt to take their life or have voiced such plans that are hospitalized. The majority will find relief over time or through Christian or professional counseling and with medication. Time itself is the most common healing agent for depression.

A great concern comes when depression lasts for weeks rather than days.

Depression can include one or more of the following symptoms:

- Persistent sad or "empty" mood

- Loss of pleasure in ordinary activities, including sex

- Decreased energy, fatigue, being "slowed down"

- Sleep disturbances (insomnia, early morning wakening, or oversleeping)

- Eating disturbances (loss of appetite and weight, or weight gain)
- Feelings of guilt, worthlessness, helplessness
- Thoughts of death or suicide, suicide attempts
- Irritability
- Excessive crying
- Chronic aches and pains that don't respond to treatment

Of course, everyone experiences one or more of these symptoms. However, when symptoms increase in number or severity or last an unusually long time, the person may be clinically depressed. Clinical depression is an illness. It is not a failure or demonic possession. Depression is labeled clinical when it needs treatment and when it is professionally identified by certain established criteria.

Is it my fault?

A doctor helped me by describing the chemical activity within my brain. When certain chemicals that facilitate the communication between brain cells diminish, depression occurs. It is similar to wiring. Many have noticed corrosion around battery terminals of their car. If this corrosion gets into the wires from the battery, no current will flow to start the engine. A long-term depression can deplete the chemical processes necessary to maintain normal brain function. Sometimes a change of pace or rest will allow the brain to produce the necessary level of chemicals needed. If this does not occur, then medication can replace the missing chemicals until the brain heals.

I like to compare this to a broken leg. I am quite sure that practical sense says a broken leg should have a cast for six weeks or more for the bones to knit together. Medication for depression is a cast for the nerve paths until the brain sufficiently produces its own chemicals in balance. When viewed practically, it is much easier to erase a fearful shunning by friends and relatives. The old dark dogma of using medication for brain functions that correspond to a psychotic condition has generally disappeared in today's world. However, uneducated or misinformed people may still have a disregard for the use of medical help for depression.

Suggest to someone in pain that it's "all in your mind," and be prepared to duck. Yet, this could be right. New research suggests that a network of nerves in the brain may determine why two people respond in dramatically different ways to what appears to be equivalent pain.

Researchers have discovered what they call a pain-enhancing system. Just as somewhat mysterious brain chemicals called *endorphins* appear to kill pain, this network of nerves seems to enhance it.

A neurologist says the pathway is particularly noticeable in patients who have taken opiates, such as morphine. Some physicians believe these drugs may beef up the pain-enhancing network, forcing addicts to take more of the drug to keep the pain down.

Researchers' next goal is to understand the chemical neurotransmitters that carry pain messages along the pathway.

That could lead to a new generation of drugs to block the chemical activity.

Do I need a psychiatrist?

I can still hear people emphatically say, "I do *not* need a psychiatrist." Whether they still cling to an old stigma of fear or pride, a psychiatrist is a medical doctor who has spent extra time and effort in the study of the brain and human mental processes. I have not asked my dentist to remove my appendix, and I am not going to ask my optometrist to help with my depression.

Why isn't faith sufficient to heal or deliver me from depression?

Faith may just be your answer. A renewed attitude of a positive relationship with the Lord does wonders. Maybe fellowship will reinforce your attitude and bring you out of a depression, but faith is limitless. Though I try to be careful, balancing faith and practical sense do not always go arm-in-arm. What many tend to forget is that their brain is an organ of the body. The root of depression is found within the brain's functions.

Again, let me compare your brain to another organ. If you recently had a meal of red-hot chili, followed by a pepperoni pizza and a bottle of soda, indigestion or a stomachache is likely to follow soon. You would not feel guilty taking some Tums, Rolaids or Maalox. Your stomach is an organ like your brain. When it is not functioning correctly, something or someone needs to intervene.

Some Christians today purport that depression is demon oppression or possession—depending upon their theology. Their teaching or beliefs may prevent them from receiving competent help. I do not dismiss the activity of Satan to lie, kill and destroy, but I know one thing: Satan is not omniscient, omnipotent nor omnipresent. To accuse him of all illnesses that are related to our mind is reckless and may preclude a dear person from receiving help. If, in the presence of qualified pastors and leaders, demonic activity is obvious—either verbally or visually—then let the wisdom of the Scriptures and Holy Spirit lead in the deliverance of the oppressed.

If you do choose to go to a psychiatrist for your first time, one thing you might notice is lack of a proverbial couch. All professional offices I have visited either as a patient or as a pastor have a desk and a couple of chairs. The setting is very similar to a pastor's office. Great attention is given to comfort and privacy. I do see a psychiatrist as part of my pain regimen. He controls and balances my required medications. During our sessions, we hold a normal conversation. He does not quiz me for answers, I provide the information he needs just by telling him how I feel.

What will people think if I see a psychiatrist?

When someone says, "My pastor will lose confidence in me if he finds out that I am seeing a doctor for mental health," I feel very comfortable in saying, "I doubt it." If your pastor has a good understanding of depression, he or she can help. A pastor's knowledge of your need will help the pastor understand why you may have not been yourself. Your pastor was used to seeing you vibrant and attending regularly. However, lately you missed some worship services or stopped teaching a class. If you feel comfortable, include your pastor or staff member in your healing process. They are a valuable resource for encouragement and reaffirming your self-worth.

As a pastor, I have counseled many in various stages of depression. I am always careful to determine whether their depression is mild, chronic or clinical. If the counselee is in clinical or near clinical depression, I refer them to a professional psychologist or psychiatrist. I have not had a person say, "No" to a referral. There are other forms of depression, which I would refer to professionals, but an explanation of their symptoms is not necessary for the scope of this book.

Some people may be afraid that their friends and relatives will find out that they are seeking professional help. This is a fear before it is a reality. Neither the professional nor you need to tell others. It would be appropriate to discuss your need with an understanding spouse or parent. If your spouse or close relative does not understand why professional help is needed, ask them to accompany you to your next appointment. Most professionals I have met encourage family understanding and participation in the healing process. Inevitably, there is the negative person who refuses to accept the need for professional or medical intervention. Once again, either the doctor or a pastor can share the process of healing from clinical depression.

Will I become addicted?

Many patients are afraid to take medication for depression because they fear addiction or other side effects. An amazing aspect of antidepressant medication is that you generally do not feel anything, and antidepressants are not addictive with prescribed use. Most of them are cumulative, which means they need to build up within your system to become effective. When they are effective, the only thing you feel is normal and for the depressed person, normal is the greatest feeling in the world.

It is important to note that your medication may be cumulative. Therefore, your medication lingers in your body after discontinuing the daily dosage. Do not do this on your own. Just because you feel normal does not mean your depression is cured. The brain takes time to restore a chemical imbalance. Medication allows the brain time to recover and produce normally.

If you stop the medication prematurely, you will feel all right for a short time, but then the depression will return. Often, it returns as a deeper depression than it was originally. Your doctor will slowly remove the medication when it has been determined that the healing has begun. Please remember to take your medication as directed, and do not make changes without consultation. You would not remove the cast of a broken leg just because it felt better. Your leg would be weak and likely break again—requiring extensive medical attention.

I should mention that exercise helps in recovering from depression. However, a depressed person ordinarily does not feel like exercise and is too tired to put in motion the activity that will help. This short humorous quote describes how a depressed person may think. "Just for today, I will not sit in my living room all day watching TV. Instead, I will move my TV into the bedroom." —Anonymous

Depression can become a vicious circle of knowing what you could or should do to help, but feeling too poorly to help yourself. Then guilt, or a sense of failure, may come and deepen your depression. This cycle can be broken by intervention and that may come from the help of friends, your pastor or medicine.

Sunlight has a direct effect on people's moods. When pastoring on the West Coast, our normally sunny city was going through a prolonged period of cloudiness and low overhead fog. In a hospital elevator, I heard one doctor say to his peer, "We are having the Seattle syndrome." They both commented regarding the greater than normal number of depressed people they were seeing. Prolonged lack of sunlight creates the "Seattle syndrome" or, for the New Englander, "cabin fever."

People who live in these climates may experience seasonal depression that comes on during or after the fall holidays and extends until spring. This is not necessarily clinical depression, but it is certainly chronic depression. I do know that some of my New England relatives followed this pattern. The large amounts of snow would prevent outside activity and contribute to the doldrums. Thankfully, each spring the daffodils pushing up through the melting snow let them know they could resume their normal activities.

> *Encouragement is like a premium gasoline—it helps to take knocks out of living*
>
> —Anonymous

What if going to church is not helping?

This may be how you, a depressed person feels, but going to church is not hurtful either. You just might meet the Healer in the next service. Your inner spirit should be lifted from the praise, worship and hearing of the Word. Do not give up on God because He will never give up on you. It is His good will that you prosper and be in good health as your soul prospers (3 John 1:2). The Psalmist David recognized that he could never be far from the presence of God.

> Where can I go from Your Spirit? Or where can I flee from Your presence? If I ascend into heaven, You *are* there; if I make my bed in hell, behold, You *are there* (Psalm 139:7, 8).

In Psalm 42, David asks, "Why are you downcast, O my soul? Why so disturbed within me?" (Psalm 42:5, *NIV*). Apparently, he was not sure of its cause. In fact, he seemed to be a bit bewildered, perhaps asking: "Why me? Why now?" *Downcast* here literally means, sink, depress, bow down, collapse or despair. *Disturbed* conveys the idea of tumult, rage, moaning, clamor or troubled.

In his battle to win over depression, the Psalmist focused on five areas:

1. *Appetite*—"As the deer pants for streams of water, so my soul pants for you, O God . . . for the living God" (Psalm 42:1, 2, *NIV*). Because nothing spoils our appetite for Him more than harboring iniquity, we may want to ask ourselves the question, "Is there any sin in my life with which I need to deal?" (Psalm 66:18; 139:23, 24; Hebrews 3:13).

2. *Commune*—"These things I remember as I pour out my soul . . . I say to God my Rock, 'Why have you forgotten me? Why must I go about mourning, oppressed by the enemy?' " (Psalm 42:4, 9, *NIV*). We may need to get on our face before God (literally) and have a real heart-to-heart talk over the issues that are troubling us at our core.

3. *Redirect*—"Put your hope in God" (vv. 5, 11, *NIV*). We may need to redirect our expectancy to Him, rather than wallow in worry, circumstances, fear or anger.

4. *Praise*—"I will yet praise him, my Savior and my God" (vv. 5, 11, *NIV*). We choose to worship Him as an alternative to complaining or experiencing self-pity (1 Corinthians 10:10; Philippians 2:14, 15).

5. *Recall*—"My soul is downcast within me; therefore I will remember you from the land of the Jordan, the heights of Hermon—from Mount Mizar" (Psalm 42:6, *NIV*). It may be time once again to recall and appreciate God's past leading and blessings. Nothing displeases God, or quenches our spirit more than a thankless heart (see Nehemiah 9:17; Psalm 63:6; 77:11; 106:7; Isaiah 46:9).

What is it like not being depressed?

If you have ever experienced a long period of depression, recovery is wonderful. Gone are the feelings of gloom and negative outlook. You once again have a feeling of self-worth, and you are no longer helpless. I remember years ago when I had gone through a period of depression, all of a sudden, I felt normal. Normal was the greatest feeling I had enjoyed in a long time. My day was brighter. The laughter of my children was pleasing, and it was great to be alive.

If you are depressed and I have encouraged you to seek help, then look forward to the day when the sun shines on your face, and His face shines through you.

> *Do all the good you can, In all the ways you can, In all the places you can, At all the times you can, To all the people you can, As long as ever you can.*
>
> —John Wesley

Reflections for Discussion

1. Some have attributed depression to demonic oppression. Is it a natural part of our humanity?

2. When should a person seek professional help for depression?

3. How do you respond to this question? "Why isn't faith sufficient to heal or deliver me from depression?"

4. Does a stigma of rejection exist today for those who seek professional help from psychiatrists or psychologists?

5. Have you ever experienced a "seasonal depression," and how long did it last?

SEVEN

I Can't Let Go

"What greater rebellion, impiety, or insult to God can there be than not to believe his promises?"

—Martin Luther

How can I live with my condition?

Do you remember the hit television show, *Hee, Haw*? If so, then you probably remember the song about gloom, despair and agony on me. The song goes on to talk about deep, dark depression and excessive misery. If it weren't for bad luck, I'd have no luck at all—just gloom, despair and agony on me. It may be remembered as a humorous lyric, yet some seem to live by its theme and glory in their ills. When in pain or living in a disabled condition, it is difficult to think of other people. To live a quality life, we should try to be positive in our trial. Sympathy may be your desired response from others. But sympathy will only be given a few times from the same person before they begin avoiding you.

If it is an attention-getting attempt, it will ultimately fail, and loneliness and exclusion will fill its place. We are misguided if we think that continually repeating our story of pain and suffering will create friendships. People with the gift of mercy are needed to minister to the depressed and lonely.

Joni and Friends Web site has a free booklet called, "Christianity With Its Sleeves Rolled Up" www.joniandfriends.org). It is based on Joni's early experiences after the shattering injury that broke her neck and left her paralyzed. This booklet is full of wisdom as she shares stories of people using their spiritual gifts to help her and her family through different needs. When she was depressed, someone with the gift of mercy would visit. She was encouraged by another who had the gift of teaching as the Scriptures opened up to her. If you have the gift of service or mercy, let the Lord direct you to someone who is waiting just for you.

I have a friend in New England who has multiple sclerosis. She is a delight to be around as she continues to raise a family and play in a family gospel group. Occasionally, she is not able to travel with her family group, but I've never heard a word of complaint. Whenever I visited with her family, there was always a spirit of joy and happiness.

A physician of mine has multiple sclerosis, but she is always a joy to visit. Her face beams with a smile, and her attitude is positive as she cares for patients who suffer from chronic pain. It causes me to do an attitude check. Would I be able to be as pleasant as my doctor is day in and day out? I hope so and will always try.

Have you noticed that a friend or relative sometimes develops the same problems? I have heard the term *sympathy pains* while an expectant father is with the mother-to-be during her labor pains. For years, I watched a situation between two very close cousins. When one cousin developed an illness, the other cousin imagined the same illness. It even went to the extent when one cousin did develop diabetes, the other was sure they had the same and purchased diabetes testing kits. They would compare blood sugar levels. If the mimicking cousin's reading was normal, there was always an excuse with the testing strips, equipment, time of day and so forth. They would compare pains and tell each other how terrible each felt. After a while, it was disencouraging to listen to their conversation.

I have met people who just enjoyed talking about themselves. Whether they have a need to draw attention to themselves or they like telling others how badly they feel; I am not sure. It may be a need to reinforce certain inner needs or desires. I personally love to speak of my wife, children, grandchildren and other historical or contemporary subjects.

Why do people like to linger with their problems?

Why can't they let go and turn their attention to productive and energizing activities? I am not able to give a definite answer, but often I have noticed that these people have a low self-esteem. Their lives appear to be unproductive and without meaning. It could be that the self-attention device is to reinforce a sense of importance to boost their ego.

Individualism has a definite place in this discussion. God did not give us all the same personality. In order to minister and help, we must always consider each person's needs, along with the environment and family life style of each.

While considering this topic, I remembered going to meetings where people would tell of their conversion, prior lifestyle or a miraculous event. They were encouraging. Then it began to seem as a competitive event, for the more impressive their testimony, the greater was God's grace. I began to compare some stories and the number of miles that were driven on an empty gas tank. An addiction story was more incredible than the last and the more horrific the crimes of the past, the greater the testimony.

Please do not think that I am implying that their testimonies were concocted. I believe they told what they knew to be the truth in their life and were joyous for the deliverance and salvation of the Lord. I am using this as an example to show how people do like to speak of suffering and ills, but the difference here is that their suffering is past, and life is changed and renewed. Rather than dwelling on the old, people give thanks for the new.

It is important to consider that as a person's health changes and other problems arrive, frustration over additional difficulties may be overwhelming.

My stepfather developed a fever and incredible pain. To his doctors, it appeared as a form of gout, and they followed a modality of treatment for gout. However, he did not improve and his pain spread. It took approximately six months to diagnose a rare form of rheumatoid arthritis that deformed his feet, ankles and knees. During a long, painful process, I never heard him utter a single word of complaint. He eventually could walk with a crutch and a cane, but the pain and damage continued for several years.

My mother called to tell me he was in the hospital with an aggressive flu, and not expected to live. He was in his late 80s; however, he did survive with an unusual side effect. The rheumatoid arthritis stopped its rampage, and his pain was gone although the prior damage remained. When he spoke, it was not of his pain, but his freedom of pain. During his long illness, it was always pleasant to be around him. I pray that I have learned from my stepfather, who is now with the Lord.

Even though I have an intrathecal pump to aid in pain relief, it is not without side effects. Its continued use causes bone loss similar to osteoporosis, lowers levels of testosterone in men that saps energy and potentially a growth could form at the end of the catheter that could cause instant paralysis. I do not dwell on these possible outcomes. Rather, I take large, daily doses of calcium, testosterone and have tests to check the catheter in my spine. I would rather deal with potential side effects than return to the agonizing pain. My pain does not control my mind. My lifestyle had changed, but I am always looking for other opportunities to minister. I know that I have bad and good days. However, I attempt not to let it affect those around me. I do not want to drive away the people I love.

I do understand the frustration of a long-term disability, and I realize that others suffer—often without answers. They may be enduring a situation similar to my stepfather. Their disease has not presented itself in such a way as to receive a definitive diagnosis. Possibly the illness is beyond the scope of a family doctor, and time is required for testing and consultation with specialists. Their pain may not respond to drug therapy. Changes in medication and balancing the effects can lead to distress. Now I can hear the complaints of a patient. The patient is no longer patient. Their life is upset from the norm, and they can no longer plan family functions.

To caregivers, I would like to offer this statement. Sometimes your loved one needs love the most when they are the most unlovable. Disease, fear of dying, loss of independence and a multitude of other concerns affect a person's attitude, and may result in a personality change. These changes may cause friction in what used to be a loving and caring relationship. Remember your loved one is sick and a godly love requires a positive response. This friction, or conflict in personality, may be new to you, but your loved one needs you even more during these difficult times. As the caregiver, you face trials and sorrows along with the one for whom you are caring.

Should I expect difficulties?

Jesus was unequivocal on this point. He did not say, "You may have trials and sorrows." He did not say, "If you stray off the right path you will have trials and sorrows." No. He says, "You will have many trials and sorrows." They will come regardless of the path.

If you know of a person who appears to glory in their sufferings, try to get them help. You might be the right person with the appropriate spiritual gift to minister. Aid them by reinforcing their understanding of God's grace and mercy. This Scripture describes it all: "And now abide faith, hope, love, these three; but the greatest of these *is* love" (1 Corinthians 13:13).

A few people have a misunderstanding of the Bible or individual scriptures. One man's suffering was his fear of the sting of death. He had heard the verse in song, from the pulpit and read it in the Bible, yet he never comprehended its correct interpretation. He was afraid that as he died, there would be terrible pain, known as "the sting of death." I was able to minister to him personally and share scriptures along with the one he feared. "O death, where *is* thy sting? O grave, where *is* thy victory?" (1 Corinthians 15:55, KJV).

He was able to recognize that the verse is asking, "Where is the sting?" and that the grave has no victory over the believer. He realized that he was a winner, and death and the grave were losers. I witnessed a visible sense of peace come over him. Later, as he came near to death, he spoke of "beings" in his room to comfort him when he was physically alone or when his daughter was the only visitor. Death came very peaceably to my friend. His family was greatly comforted knowing he no longer feared death, but accepted it gracefully.

Life is a miracle; it is not something to suffer through. If you find yourself concentrating on your problems and sickness, reach out and accept love and encouragement from others. There is a purpose in living. Many do not have any idea of what their purpose is, but it is very simple. Your purpose in life is to glorify God by what you do, say and think. Try to bring into line, not only your outward actions and verbalizations, but surrender your thoughts to the Holy Spirit. He will bring you comfort in your need.

> *We turn to God for help when our foundations are shaking only to learn that it is God shaking them.*
>
> —Charles West

In addition, we are to be thankful in the midst of a situation. I reiterate this basic concept because it is the Word of God to apply to our lives in all situations. Paul did not say, "If things are going your way, be thankful." He said no matter what happens, be thankful. "In every thing give thanks: for this is the will of God in Christ Jesus concerning you" (1 Thessalonians 5:18, KJV).

> *Remember that the song from "Hee, Haw" was in jest. It was never intended as a living standard. Our words should be as quoted by Norman Vincent Peale: "Never talk defeat. Use words like hope, belief, faith, victory."*
>
> —Norman Vincent Peale
> Positive Thinking Every Day

Reflections for Discussion

1. Why do people like to linger with their problems?

2. "Sometimes your loved one needs love the most when they are the most unlovable." What does this mean to you?

3. What do trials and sorrows mean?

4. How can a person be thankful when immersed in life's difficulties?

5. What is your purpose in life?

6. Describe those things that give your life real purpose.

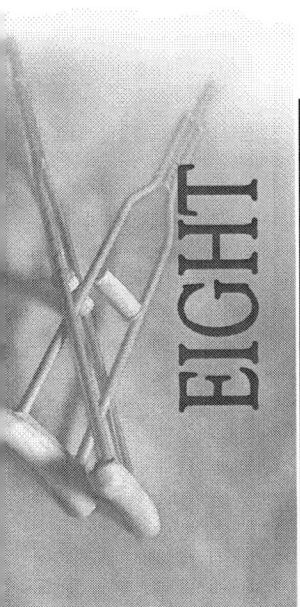

EIGHT

My Loved One Died!

God gave us memories that we might have roses in December.

—Sir James Barrie

What about the pain of loss?

One of the most harmful statements regarding loss is "time heals all wounds." Once again, people measure healing with time. The loss of a loved one and the grief process are not on a timeline. Time is part of the action of grief recovery but not the definitive rule.

There is a greater sense of loss at the sudden death of a healthy parent, spouse or child, which does not lessen the importance of others who die after a lengthy illness. When death strikes up-close and personal, shock, anger, grief, depression and eventually, acceptance, are feelings that will become a real part of life. Death either has or will come into everyone's life, but it is not a defeat.

On the contrary, for a believer, it is victory that leads to our eternal home.

I have mentioned earlier that my wife and I lost our first child. I would like to fill in the missing pictures of that story in this chapter.

There had been nothing abnormal during Lee Ann's pregnancy. She had visited her obstetrician according to schedule and our baby was well. In April, Lee Ann experienced a day of discomfort that continued through the night. I called her doctor and soon, we were on our way to the hospital 15 miles away. With my emergency lights flashing, people pulled to the side of the road to let us through traffic. We arrived at the hospital, and Lee Ann was rushed to the delivery room.

Escorted to a small room, I waited, not knowing what was happening. Soon a blood-covered doctor entered and told me that our child was alive, but due to her premature arrival, she was not expected to live. I spent the next two hours with my wife until we were notified that our baby had passed away. I signed a birth and death certificate at the same time. We named her Susan. We were both 22 years old when we lost our baby.

Because the ground in Maine was still frozen, it would be a couple of months before we could bury our daughter. A local funeral home was gracious to us and held her body until the cemetery could receive her. Lee Ann and I were alone in our grief. Our relatives did not come to see us. My classmates and fraternity brothers were mute. It was difficult to understand why we had lost our first child. Although we were believers, we were not members of a church, so there was no support or encouragement.

In late May, the ground had thawed enough that a small grave could be prepared. We owned a '70 Volkswagen and those of you who are familiar with VW's know there is a small space behind the back seat. My wife and I drove first to the funeral parlor, where I was handed a small casket similar in size to a picnic cooler, which fit in the space behind the back seat.

Then we drove an hour and a half to our hometown cemetery where two young men had dug a grave. It was raining as I placed Susan's casket in the ground and had a moment of silence and prayer. Picture a young father and mother burying their baby alone, with no pastor present, no family or friends. Please do not let another couple go through that agony and loneliness if you can help.

Grief, though a personal process, should include family members, friends and clergy helping those who have lost a part of their life. The survivor is going to feel loss for their child, sibling, spouse or parent, along with loss of control, and maybe disappointment with God. Their grief may be expressed in physical sensations, feelings, and outcries of pain or sobbing.

Isn't grief often labeled as "a working through"?

If we label grief as work, then it can be broken down into the following tasks:

1. Recognizing that your loved one is dead and will not return.

2. Allowing yourself to experience and express your feelings.

3. Finding a place in thoughts for memories.

4. Adjusting to life as a single, if appropriate.

5. Readjusting life according to your own desires and interests.

6. Encouraging a surviving spouse to pay attention to the process of grief rather than trying to hurry on to a new life.

Have you heard that it takes two years to "get over" the death of a loved one; five years to "get over" the death of a parent; and you never "get over" the death of a child? You would never forget a child who had died, anymore than you would ever forget a parent or a loved one. The key here once again is use of the word *time*. It is the actions within time that lead to successful grief recovery.

When a loss occurs, whatever the tragedy, a person dealing with loss might grapple with these questions:

- "Why would God allow this?"

- "When will I heal?"

- "Will God really use this situation for my good?"

- "How will I rebuild?"

The interview in this next section describes how one man dealt with a great personal tragedy.

❝ *Death ends a life, not a relationship.* ❞

—Jack Lemmon

The following is an interview with my friend the Reverend David S. Bishop, Ph.D. In 1964 while driving with her two small daughters, Dave's wife, Shirley Yvonne Orndorff Bishop, was in an auto accident. Their two girls were relatively unharmed, but Shirley was grievously injured. Hundreds of friends and family prayed during the time Shirley was in the hospital. For eight days she was maintained on life support, though in all likelihood, she was clinically dead the majority of the time. She was 23 years old.

At the time, Dave was an instructor at West Coast Bible College in Fresno, California. The death of his young wife left him widowed with two little girls—2 and 4 years old. Although he was fortunate to have a community of support, his remarks reveal a sense of deep loss and suppressed grief. These are his words:

> "I was a young man though I thought of myself as being quite mature. I was really young in the faith and in my way of looking at things. Looking back, it was a tough blow, a real tough blow. As best I could, I looked at it idealistically and theologically, though I was probably not very theologically correct. My motivation was that people would be looking at me as if my faith was on trial. Frankly, there was a lot of

denial, not that she was dead, but that grief should be a part of the process.

At the funeral for example, I kissed her goodbye in the casket, yet I never shed a tear. Feeling that my faith was on trial, I reasoned, 'Why should I grieve when she is so much better off?' But, while all that was true, after about two weeks, it collapsed on me. Grief is a progression where you might feel high motivation to be strong, but you still have to go through the pain. Grief is a process that you have to go through and when you think you are through it, you have not gotten there yet."

When you said you collapsed, what did you feel?

"I just felt pain from the loss. I had two little girls, and my thoughts of them caused reality to set in. They were 2 and 4 at the time and I would have to provide for them. Shirley's mother and father moved in, and that worked for a little while. Later, they returned to their home, and I had an elderly lady move in to take care of the girls."

You had mentioned to me previously that you became very lonely.

"After many months, you live with the loss, but you are aware of being very lonely. At the time, I was with a cultural group that would not accept my looking at another woman for at least a year after the loss of one, but that is an unrealistic expectation. For example, pastors might ask me to come preach in their church because they had a young woman they wanted me to meet. That never worked very well either, because I didn't desire that kind of help."

How did you feel emotionally when looking at your children? They must have brought back some emotions of grief.

"A lot of things can trigger grief. The girls would be one thing that would trigger it; however, now things with my old crowd had changed. They were married, I wasn't, and things just didn't seem to fit anymore. You feel like a fifth wheel. Coming home to an empty house and the loneliness of going to bed at night also triggered the grief. Of course, the children were there, and that made the loss very real. So, any number of things can trigger grief. For instance, six months of decent experiences go by, then something happens and you have a relapse. It may even be a year. That is one of the things I think most people are unprepared for. For me, it happened even after two years. It was not a process of denial and I did not blame God, but the pain was real and the loss was real."

You never asked "Why?"

"No, not really, because if indeed I am His and all things are working together for good, as painful as this is, there has to be a reason and I am going to love God through it. While that sounds a little idealistic, it's really not. I was not sophisticated in my thinking, but that is basically where I was."

Several years following the death of his wife, Dave married Sandra Alyn Reasy. They added another girl and boy to his existing family. Sandra has been a loving mother to all four children and David's wife for 38 years.

> *Death is no more than passing from one room into another. But there's a difference for me, you know. Because in that other room I shall be able to see.*
>
> —Helen Keller

Because of David's strong belief, he never struggled with the sovereignty and providence of God or the problem of evil and human suffering. An unbeliever on the other hand, might question God and ask, "Why?" Just telling them that God allowed it for a purpose may not be enough to help. An encouraging personality with consistent and constant support will help them deal with these issues.

How long should the grief process last?

You may wonder when your life will be normal again, and how long is it going to take the pain to leave. Often, our expectations (and the expectations of others) are that we should move on and get our lives back. However, it is important to let the grief process do its healing. Before anyone can rebuild, he or she must realize that it takes time to rearrange the embers and splinters of tragedy. This involves surrendering your hurt, along with your healing, to God. He is the only One who can heal and make us new.

An example of allowing time for grief may be in the form of a father's or husband's favorite chair. The children may think that if they remove the chair, mother will feel better, and it will not remind her of Dad. It is best to let Mom say when it is time to move his chair. She alone knows when that part of her grief process has passed. I cannot emphasize the necessity of allowing the grief process to proceed. The one person who will know when the grief process is nearing an end or has passed is the griever. It hurts others to see people in grief, but it is a healing process and that takes time. There is no fixed schedule for this process. It may take two years or more for relapses to pass.

There are no absolutes. Grieving does not have definitive stages or time limitations. It may help to place feelings with memories or objects. These feelings do not need to be historic or involve tears. What is important is that the feelings be heart-felt and not contrived as an exercise or a suggestion from a second party.

According to Russell P. Friedman, John W. James and The Grief Recovery Institute, what grievers want most and need to do is to discuss *what happened*, and to recall their relationship with the person who died or to whom they were married.

Richard Exley describes the grieving process as "the tides of grief." These tides of grief will come in and go out. You will experience times of intense grief, followed by periods of relative calm. Then the tide will come in again, and once more you grieve. Just as suddenly, the tide will go out again so that if you did not know better, you would think you were finally over your grief. Of course, you are not. This is just another "resting period" before you resume your "grief work."

"As grief does its healing work, you will begin to notice some faint changes. When the tide of grief rolls in, it will not come in quite so far, or it will not stay as long. When it rolls back, it will go out farther and stay out longer. Your times of grief will become shorter and less powerful, while your times of respite will become longer and more renewing."

Often when I am presiding as the pastor at a funeral, I like to recite part of an old Southern gospel song. The first and second verses are as follows:

> "Death is an appointment that we all must keep,
> But as child of God, we do not die we simply fall asleep.
> To be carried away on angels wings up to heaven's door.
> Where we move into a mansion there and live forever more."

> "It hurt us all to see mother go, to be gone forever more.
> But before she closed her eyes in death, she heard a knock upon the door.
> We opened up the door for her and though we could not see,
> She said a band of angels just walked in to take me home to glory."

Chorus

> "Grave where is your victory, Death where is your sting?
> We do not die but move on high to live with Christ, our King.
> To walk on gold and see the sights untold and with the saints of old to sing,
> Grave where is your victory, Death where is your sting?"

Everything dies, but not everything ends. Death is an opening to a new life. The realities of this life cloud the view of heaven. When we lose a loved one, our world shakes. Life as we knew it has come to a stop. All the things we did seem insignificant compared to the pain we now know. Facing the reality of death causes everyone to stop and reconsider his or her own life. The opportunity to present a Savior is rich when someone has an empty hole that needs filling.

God Said . . .

I said, "God, I hurt."
And God said, "I know."

I said, "God, I cry a lot."
And God said, "That is why I gave you tears."

I said, "God, I am so depressed."
And God said, "That is why I gave you sunshine."

I said, "God, life is so hard."
And God said, "That is why I gave you loved ones."

I said, "God, my loved one died."
And God said, "So did mine."

I said, "God, it is such a loss."
And God said, "I saw mine nailed to a cross."

I said, "God, but your loved one lives."
And God said, "So does yours."

I said, "God, where are they now?"
And God said, "Mine is on My right and yours is in the Light."

I said, "God, it hurts."
And God said, "I know."

—Anonymous

Reflections for Discussion

1. Does time heal all wounds?

2. What are some reactions you have noticed when a loved one dies?

3. What types of support were missing during the author's loss of his first child?

4. Briefly discuss the interview with David Bishop. How would you handle the sudden loss of a spouse?

5. Reflect on Richard Exley's description of the grieving process as "the tides of grief."

NINE

I Have Met Job's Friends

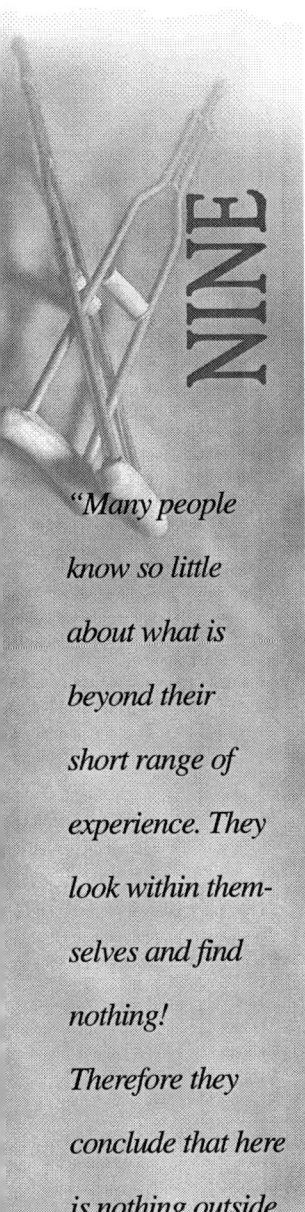

"*Many people know so little about what is beyond their short range of experience. They look within themselves and find nothing! Therefore they conclude that here is nothing outside themselves either.*"

—Helen Keller

Has televangelism affected local churches?

Have you noticed that healthy, charismatic speakers with multimedia liturgical formats and multifaceted, music ministry pastor the large or mega churches in North America? Forty years ago there were some very large churches, although the norm was a congregation of 60 to 200 people with a senior pastor, maybe an assistant for the youth and a secretary. One contributing factor to this change has been televangelism. It has affected viewers' attitudes and perceptions of the local church. Many churches have fashioned their worship service after a television style of a variety show.

Televangelism has affected many evangelicals' theology. The *Word-faith* or health-wealth movements spread extensively through tapes and best-selling books. In some cases, televangelism helped popularize various versions of a Biblical view of the end times. There have been waves of emphasis that a popular televangelist might introduce, and local churches would adopt as their service topic. I call these waves because their emphasis would change with a degree of regularity. In many ways, it has benefited our modern church, but at the same time has placed unrealistic expectations on congregations and pastoral staff.

Unless a pastor keeps up with the times or the recent wave, some church attendees become listless and seek the perfect church, which we know they will never find. The pastor finds it necessary to represent a model of health and success. I agree wholeheartedly that the pastor should be a role model. He walks a difficult path wherein he is allowed his humanity, but his spiritual life must be above question. Difficulty arises when his spiritual life is measured by his health.

Why does a congregation want a healthy pastor?

For some, it is an indication of strength. He exudes confidence to his flock who recognize their own frailties. A pastor with a continuing illness appears to some a sign of weakness. A pastor who requires continued use of medicine may be seen as a person of lesser faith. Often during an illness, a faction of a church will attempt to assume leadership and seek to remove the pastor. Others might question his faith. I mentioned earlier in this book that a member asked me if I was qualified to preach on faith when I have not been healed. Do you remember my answer in Chapter 2?

A few years ago, due to personal and medical factors, I came near to death. The stress of taking care of two dying parents, a church and my own pain extracted severe damage to my health. After a period of recovery, a group of members prevented me from preaching from the pulpit to which I had been assigned. I did not lose just my parents, but I also lost my church. Thankfully, many stepped in to care for me as I returned to health and ministry. Members of my local congregation saw to our physical needs and my denomination provided a time of recovery and restoration. I mention this to point out my experience with expectations of a congregation and the state of health of its pastor.

By no means is my experience a normal response; however, it is not uncommon. At the other end of the topic is an overwhelming number of churches full of care and grace. I read of a pastor with cerebral palsy who was pastoring a church with attendance in excess of 1,000 during the 1980's. His church showed the compassion of Christ in its acceptance of him, regardless of his health. I personally knew a neighboring pastor who had heart disease, and his church supported and kept him through his surgeries and recovery.

Christians will let us down at some of our most critical and difficult times. Jesus learned this the hard way. When He was arrested without an indicted crime and soon to be killed on a cross, all the disciples and His dearest friends ran away. They left Him in His time of need and darkest hour.

Though Christians may fail you, this does not mean that God forgets you. He does not. He has a plan for you. In the middle of all your heartbreak and suffering, tell God, "I'm going to hold on and wait for You to show me Your kindness and Your love, no matter what happens."

You will be able to say what the Psalmist said, "Wait on the Lord; be of good courage, and He shall strengthen your heart; wait, I say, on the Lord!" (Psalm 27:14).

Have I met Job's friends?

Yes, I have. Some have been well-meaning in their attempts to console and counsel. Others have shown a lack of comfort and compassion. Some had their own agendas and worked against the leadership.

Consider healing in the life and time of Christ's ministry. People could have faith in healing because they saw the dead rise and the blind see. Healing was visible and expected. The area of difficulty for people of Christ's life was salvation. They could not believe that a man could forgive sin. Today, we find it easy to believe in forgiveness of sin for we know Who took our sins away. Healing is harder for us to believe and understand in our time, as it is not often visibly seen. This area of faith must find its support in God's Word.

> For I will restore health to you and heal you of your wounds," says the Lord, "Because they called you an outcast saying: 'This is Zion; no one seeks her' (Jeremiah 30:17).

Job's friends of today are not very different other than their solutions. There are those who point to your need for forgiveness in order to receive your healing. Forgiveness is a good start, but it may not be your key to healing. Others may want to drive out a demon. This might be correct if a demon is indeed the source of your illness. However, there might not be any demonic activity present. Then there are the health lifestyle proponents with herbs and potions sure to cure all. Some will recommend a certain book or their choice of scriptures. Others say more personal prayer is needed or suggest that church attendance has not been regular enough.

The majority of the responses from Job's friends in Scripture was that there was sin or guilt in his life. Eliphaz is a venerable and devout elder who, with his eminent depth of insight, adds a longing compassion. Eliphaz' major point was that people do not suffer without a cause. Experience had taught him that affliction was God's punishment for sin. These scriptures summarize his view.

> Remember now, who *ever* perished being innocent? Or where were the upright *ever* cut off? Even as I have seen, those who plow iniquity and sow trouble reap the same. By the blast of God they perish, and by the breath of His anger they are consumed (Job 4:7-9).

Bildad, from the community of Shuah, was a hard-nosed traditionalist. He was more as a scholar steeped in the role of inflexible tradition. He pushed aside Job's protestations of innocence as "strong wind" (8:2). He even said that Job's children had died as punishment for sin. These words of comfort did not fit a man who had faithfully sacrificed offerings on behalf of his children.

> So it was, when the days of feasting had run their course, that Job would send and sanctify them, and he would rise early in the morning and offer burnt offerings *according to* the number of them all. For Job said, "It may be that my sons have sinned and cursed God in their hearts." Thus Job did regularly (1:5).

Bildad assumed Job's source of terrible guilt lay in his past.

> If you *were* pure and upright, Surely now He would awake for you, And prosper your rightful dwelling place (8:6).

Zophar of Naamah was arrogant in his religious attack. He was more impulsive and rigid, with a dogmatist's trait of intolerance. He was a man of great morals; therefore, he could see Job's problem. He reasoned that because God is limitless and almighty, He "knows deceitful men" (11:11). Therefore, if Job would put away his evil, God would restore him. "If iniquity were in your hand, and you put it far away, and would not let wickedness dwell in your tents;" (v. 14).

Elihu, a young Aramean who speaks after the others, is portrayed with a young man's positive and absolute conviction, and with it a self-conceit that overwhelms his ability. Elihu acknowledged that he was with men older and wiser than he (32:6-9). He pointed out that when Job had protested his innocence, no one had proven him guilty. "I paid close attention to you; and surely not one of you convinced Job, or answered his words" (v. 12).

He went on to suggest that a person who is suffering may not be enduring punishment but may be receiving a call to uprightness.

> Then He opens the ears of men, And seals their instruction. In order to turn man from his deed, and conceal pride from man, He keeps back his soul from the Pit, and his life from perishing by the sword (33:16-18).

Job's friends spent days telling Job that his suffering was his own fault. Certain of their own ideas and dogma of right, wrong, justice and God, they never took time to consider Job's feelings. They never thought they might be doing more harm than good.

As humans, we want our world and God neat, orderly and easy to understand. Do not throw the unexpected at us. Instead, give us an explanation for our sidetracks of life. We do not want a God who does things that are confusing or upsetting. We like formulas that are easy to repeat with a convenient set of rules, regulations and attitudes. To have God not always act according to what we understand of Him is disconcerting as was the case with Job's friends.

The Book of Job does not give us clear answers, nor does it allow us to say, "I've got it. I know what it means." Suffering is full of mysteries that defy our simple answers. It is true that mysteries remain and some things are over our head. This is not a comfortable position to be in because it defies our inner needs. However, God has not left us solely on our own. Responding in a personable manner to God is our best answer to suffering. Allow Him to be sovereign and realize that nothing can separate us from His love.

> *God whispers in our pleasures but shouts in our pain. Pain is His megaphone to rouse a dulled world.*
>
> —C.S. Lewis

Adversity in the form of trials and trouble is good for us in that it reminds us of our need for the Comforter. When others do not think well of us or understand our need, we are more inclined to seek God who sees our hearts. Saddened by loss, we are driven to prayer and our need for a closer walk with our Lord. Our adversity then teaches us how to relate and minister to others. We can learn from Job's friends that we know some things regarding God, although not every detail. Therefore, we cannot assume we know what God is doing in others' lives. Rather than increase their suffering, we must be a light of hope and joy.

> *Comfort and prosperity have never enriched the world as much as adversity has.*
>
> —Billy Graham

Reflections for Discussion

1. How has televangelism had an effect on worship style, liturgy and congregational expectations?

2. Why does a congregation want a healthy pastor?

3. When "let down" or deserted in a time of need, what hurts the most, the problem or the friend?

4. Like the author, have you ever met "Job's friends"?

5. Why do we like formulas, a convenient set of rules, regulations and attitudes that are easy to repeat?

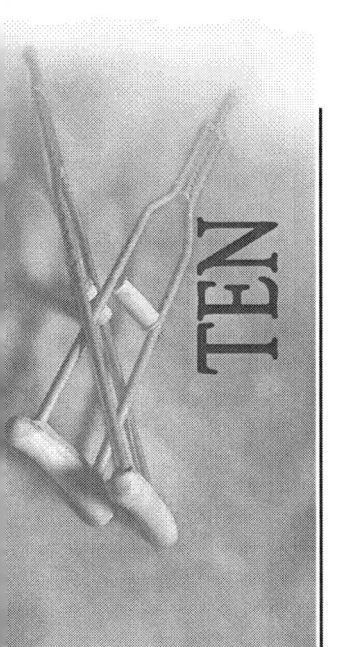

TEN

His Burden, My Blessing

*Look around you
Be distressed.*

*Look within you.
Be depressed.*

*Look at Jesus.~
Be at rest!*

—Corrie ten Boom

Do you still seek healing?

Our Lord told us to give Him our labor and rest when He said, "Come to Me, all you who labor and are heavy laden, and I will give you rest" (Matthew 11:28). He takes our burdens and gives us freedom from sins past and forgiveness for wrong choices in our future. I prefer His burden and am pleased to surrender my own. He said that His burden is light.

> Take My yoke upon you and learn from Me, for I am gentle and lowly in heart, and you will find rest for your souls. For My yoke is easy and My burden is light (vv. 29, 30).

Knowing that you are not alone in pain and sickness should give you strength of mind and spirit. You were never meant to be alone, but to be partnered with the Son of God and His Holy Spirit. You are not supposed to be under a heaviness of disappointment but rather an expectation of God's work.

Physical healing through the miraculous is somewhat similar to searching for the fountain of youth. Our problem with the fountain of youth is that it does not exist and will not be found on earth. What can be found on earth is peace of mind. There is no question that God still heals today. Many people can attest to this fact. However, there are thousands still seeking their healing by traveling to special services, evangelists, seminars and purchasing books, tapes and videos. Others will spend hundreds of thousands of dollars seeking "the cure." Then there is a combination of both who seek healing by faith and pursue a medical solution.

I belong to the last group. I would love a miraculous healing, but until that occurs, I will still go to physicians. My prayer is for His will to be perfect in my life, as I do not like to dwell on my pain. As Corrie ten Boom noted, "If I look to myself I would be depressed."

It is difficult enough without adding more to my health issues. I mention my personal difficulty because of my familiarity; however, I do not wish to exclude the multitude of people suffering pain from burns, accidents, disease and those men and women wounded in their country's service.

The fact is that my pain is based on a series of events and physical deformities, which are not outwardly visible. These deformities are congenital, along with a genetic tendency to form blood clots, arthritic growths at a young age and other various internal abnormalities. I am not alone with deformities. Many people possess visible or internal congenital deformities, but those with internal deformities are often misguided spiritually by well-meaning but uninformed friends and relatives. On the outside, we may look normal, but inside there are defects or congenital deformities. These do not necessarily cause problems in themselves, although they may add to a physician's difficulty in treatment or surgery.

My problems started when I fell down my grandparent's stairs, and on the same day, fell six feet onto a pile of rocks—spine first in both falls. Rather than forming solid fused bone, my body has absorbed the surgically inserted fusion material. Due to the loss of fusion, hardware (namely screws) becomes loosened, which causes significant pain. In addition, arthritis attacks with bone spurs and inflammation increases the pain.

Another aspect of my pain is the nerve damage caused by injury, arthritis and surgery. A neurosurgeon once described nerve damage in a vivid and easy-to-understand manner. He asked if I remembered the paper straws we used to receive with our school lunch years ago. Each straw was round until a couple of sucks on it caused it to flatten. Once flattened, no matter how hard you tried, you could not get your straw round again. It was useless and discarded. Nerves in our body are similar to straws. In their healthy form, they have a round shape. When damaged, a nerve is flattened and will not return to its normal shape. This damage may be surgically aided, but for me surgery has not corrected my problem, and intense pain persists.

Disease affects more than the particular "diseased" part of one's anatomy: It affects, the whole body. I spent a chapter discussing depression and its coexistence with pain and suffering. There is another negative feeling that may or may not accompany depression.

> *If you want to be miserable, think about yourself, about what you want, what you like, what respect people ought to pay you and what people think of you.*
>
> —Charles Kingsley

Negative feelings may be induced by a sense of physical failure or despair due to loss of control over one's destiny. In addition, suffering or sickness includes a social factor. This ranges from assuming a sick role, therefore being free from certain routine duties and responsibilities, to becoming disconnected and isolated from the world. An individual may feel unfulfilled and diminished in life's rewards. For this reason, we see that Jesus' healing ministry was concerned not just with physical healing, but the healing of relationships—chiefly with God.

It is during our prehealing time and restorations of relationships that anxiety (preexistent or new) may enter. People are "fixated" on their health. A person starts to worry obsessively or gets lost in personal questions of "what if." Some may equate this state with a lack of faith. Many times, we are told not to worry; everything will turn out all right. Perhaps you remember a song from the 1980's that says, "Don't Worry, Be Happy." It didn't describe our times and lifestyle pressures of everyday life, much less those dealing with pain.

Do you understand the "what if" question?

At night, have you laid in bed wondering what might happen if your house caught fire? How will your children be saved? Here are some more. I am sick, what if it is cancer? How will I live if I lose my job? If my wife or husband dies, how will I support my family?

Given the stresses of modern life, it is normal to experience occasional anxiety. However, people with anxiety syndrome or panic disorder, suffer from persistent worry and tension. High levels of anxiety associated with panic disorder make ordinary activities difficult—or even impossible. Symptoms of anxiety syndrome may include the following symptoms:

- Rapid heartbeat, heart palpitations or rapid pulse rate
- Obsessive, racing, or "what-if" thoughts
- Feeling detached from yourself or feelings of unreality
- Sweating, trembling, shaking or spinning sensations
- Dizziness, feeling faint, or intense fatigue
- Nausea, constipation, or abdominal discomfort
- Chills or hot flashes
- Feelings of tingling or numbness
- Feelings of choking or suffocation
- Fear of dying

- Fear of going crazy
- Chest pain
- Shortness of breath
- Fear of losing control
- Exaggerated anxious thoughts [1]

These symptoms describe feelings that most people will feel during their life, but anxiety syndrome may be diagnosed as having two or more panic attacks followed by at least one month of worry over having another attack. Those who suffer from anxiety disorder are convinced they have an undiagnosed illness, even after medical tests come back negative.

The main symptom is an exaggerated or unfounded state of worry and anxiety, often involving such matters as health, money, family or work. Although people may realize their anxiety is excessive or unwarranted, they are unable to "snap out of it." For them, the mere thought of getting through their day can provoke anxiety. Anxiety syndrome can be difficult to diagnose because symptoms will vary from person to person, and the patient does not need to have all the symptoms listed above. Some patients go to their physician first because of stress-related complaints, such as headaches or problems sleeping.

Why Should We Be Free of Anxiety?

Is it because God does not like anxious people? Is anxiety synonymous with a lack of faith and therefore sinful? Is it because anxiety serves no useful function in our human emotional makeup? These are difficult questions. Anxiety is a riddle with many symptoms. While some of the symptoms are treatable, we still do not fully understand its function or purpose.

While worry is an undesirable disorder, anxiety seems to direct us to some bigger and constructive purposes. A certain amount of anxiety is essential. Consider a mother's concerns over her newborn baby. Is it breathing normal? Is it getting enough milk? These anxious thoughts are normal and aide the mother.

Like pain that warns of disease and damage, some anxiety is also an important warning system. Anxiety sends important messages of pending threats or danger to our emotional health. On the other hand, people who have no anxiety are dangerous; they tend to feel no guilt. This would not be a healthy way to live.

There is evidence that the high demands and stress of modern life are distorting our anxiety warning systems. Similar to depression, chemical enzymes in the brain keep us at peace when there is no danger or enable us to act in an appropriate manner when in danger. These enzymes become depleted in our overworked brains, which leads to a high incidence of debilitating, meaningless anxiety disorders. Unnecessary worry is what Jesus warns us to avoid:

> Therefore I say to you, do not worry about your life, what you will eat or what you will drink; nor about your body, what you will put on. Is not life more than food and the body more than clothing? (Matthew 6:25).

How do we overcome anxiety?

Even with medications and therapy available to us today, many Christian leaders are concerned how this problem is approached. We know that massive amounts of tranquilizers are not the solution. At the same time, the incidence of anxiety syndrome is on the rise. Over 19 million Americans suffer from an anxiety disorder today.[2] It is estimated that one in four people will experience an anxiety disorder during their lifetime. As a result, scores of people in every neighborhood suffer from persistent anxiety-related problems—difficulty in sleeping, stomach problems and generalized stress. They worry themselves into an early grave or fret away their life seeking escape through alcohol, drugs or even compulsive shopping.

Medications that calm nerves or relax muscles are helpful and necessary in panic attacks and generalized anxiety. Sufferers from these forms of anxiety disturbance need professional help. The sooner they are treated, the less likely the problem will become permanent.

Medications are useful in controlling fears, reducing stress and susceptibility to anxiety. In the end, the problem with all anxiety is a problem of lifestyle, a matter of goals and priorities. No matter how effective treatment is, the problem will recur if major life changes are not made. Along with medication and therapy, lifestyle will change if we learn to rest in the Lord and rely on His Word: ". . . casting all your care upon Him, for He cares for you" (1 Peter 5:7). The *NIV* uses the word *anxiety* in place of *care*. So give Him your anxiety, and when you give it to Him, let it go.

For some, giving up is as difficult as taking a bone away from a dog. However, a trained Setter or Retriever will drop a bird or toy at your feet. While I do not seriously compare human tendencies to those of dogs, this illustration helps to show that self-training is imperative. Self-training involves trusting in the Lord and continuing in the Scriptures. Look to the lives of the apostles. After Jesus ascended to heaven, they traveled into dangerous countries, faced murderers and shipwrecks and were not accepted in communities. Most people today would rather stay home than face the obstacles the apostles encountered. The main difference is that the apostles knew their purpose. You have a purpose, and it is to glorify God in your body.

Your blessing is to receive His peace. Take time to read a Scripture, and then meditate on it. Close your eyes and place yourself in the picture the scripture represents. See yourself with the Lord, and feel His touch as He cares for you. Listen to His words of comfort, and allow the Holy Spirit to minister to you.

How does someone's faith in Jesus Christ relate to anxiety?

It would be reckless to say that it was a form of spiritual failure. Separation and generalized anxiety may have roots that go back to early childhood and may even have genetic causes. These forms of anxiety require the skill of a well-trained professional. A well-meaning but uneducated person trying to help could significantly add to the problem.

Whatever the type of anxiety, the Christian life is well designed to help us deal with it. Achieving a balanced life is the goal. Whether or not medication is used, we must not ignore the intense effect that spiritual qualities can have on our emotional well-being. Prayer and Scripture are more than just spiritual resources. They control how we feel, our values and priorities. Nowhere does a balanced spiritual life affect us more than in the area of our anxieties.

I am convinced that one reason so many people suffer from acute anxiety today is that they fail to make this important connection. Not even our most sophisticated medical or psychological system can free us from an important part of our life, our need to connect with our Creator. This need supersedes all others, and, when it is unmet, there is good reason for anxiety.

Because many worldly therapists ignore this reality, they tend to place too much emphasis on the physical world as a cause of anxiety and fail to recognize deeper spiritual needs. Your therapist needs to be a spiritual person who understands your spiritual, along with your physical needs. There is a need for balance in all things—lifestyle, career, family and spiritual life.

> "And do not seek what you should eat or what you should drink, nor have an anxious mind. For all these things the nations of the world seek after, and your Father knows that you need these things. But seek the kingdom of God, and all these things shall be added to you" (Luke 12:29-31).

❝ *The more you reaffirm who you are in Christ, the more your behavior will begin to reflect your true identity!* ❞

—From *Victory Over the Darkness,*
Dr. Neil Anderson

Endnotes

[1] Source: National Institute of Mental Health Web site *http://www.nimh.nih.gov/publicat/anxiety.cfm#anx1*

[2] Source: National Institute of Mental Health Web site *http://www.nimh.nih.gov/publicat/anxresfact.cfm*

Reflections for Discussion

1. Corrie ten Boom's quotation at the chapter's beginning is profound. What does it say to you?

2. How does a major illness or chronic difficulty affect an individual?

3. Have you ever experienced a panic attack?

4. Is anxiety synonymous with a lack of faith, and, therefore sinful?

5. Is it difficult to rest upon this scripture? ". . . casting all your care upon Him, for He cares for you" (1 Peter 5:7).

ELEVEN

Some of My Heroes

"Courage is contagious. When a brave man takes a stand, the spines of others are often stiffened."

—Billy Graham

It was night when I drove into the parking lot of a nursing home to visit for the first time a woman named Ruth. The interior of the nursing home was a dark and dirty yellow that caused feelings of depression and drear. I found her room and looked in to see a small woman, curled up in a fetal position on an unmade bed. I spoke her name, and she turned over to look at me. I told her that I was from her church and had come to say hello and have a time of prayer. She smiled and slowly brought herself to a semi-reclined position. I could tell she was in a great amount of pain, but she was so happy to have a visitor, that she did not allow her discomfort to interrupt our time together.

"Why are you in here?" I asked.

She responded, "I cooked a big meal for a family gathering last Saturday. My nephew gave me a hug of love and broke three of my ribs."

Ruth's severe osteoporosis was so bad that a simple handshake would break bones. She loved her family and felt sorry for her nephew. He did not realize how easy it was to damage his beloved tiny aunt. He just wanted to show her his love. I asked her how she was feeling now, and she told me a story.

Lessons from Ruth

"When you make a cake, the individual parts of the recipe do not taste good. When you mix the ingredients together, it still doesn't taste good. However, after it has been in the oven, the cake is delicious. It is that way with me," she said. "I have a lot of pain, but when the trial is over, I will come forth like pure gold."

I was filled with a sense of awe as this tiny, delicate woman in a dingy and dark room spoke of the greatness of her Savior. Ruth taught me a beautiful lesson in grace that evening. Not one word of complaint was heard, just her love of God. We spoke a little longer and shared a time of prayer.

As I left her room, I no longer noticed the depressing colors and smells of the nursing home. Rather, I had a renewed sense of God's love and reason for being His minister. Ruth is with her Savior now. Her life and testimony will linger in my memory and with all who knew this wonderful handmaiden of the Lord.

Another hero is Terry Fox of Canada.

Terry lost his leg to cancer when he was a teenager. While in the hospital receiving chemotherapy, he was affected by the amount of suffering in the cancer ward and decided that, in his words, "Somewhere the hurting must stop." He decided to run across Canada to raise funds for cancer research in his home country. During his run, the "Marathon of Hope," Terry ran 28 to 30 miles a day on one real leg and one artificial leg.

He discovered halfway across his country, outside Thunder Bay Ontario, the cancer had spread to his lungs. A few months later, he died. During the run, he lifted a nation through his courage and tenacity. His pain was pushed aside to help others. To this day, every first weekend in September, there is a Terry Fox Run. There is also a mountain named after him in the Canadian Rockies and a huge memorial to him outside Thunder Bay.

Billy Graham's Story

The American evangelist and charismatic preacher, Billy Graham, became a leading spokesman for Fundamentalism when he initiated a series of tours of the United States and Europe that led to large-scale evangelism.

William Franklin Graham Jr. was born November 7, 1918, on a dairy farm near Charlotte, North Carolina. His paternal grandfather, Crook Graham, bought the farm after serving in the Confederate Army. Billy would read from his collection of history books. He also practiced baseball when finished with his chores, because his ambition was to become a professional baseball player.

When he was 16, Billy was converted and began a lifelong commitment to an evangelical career. Graham was ordained a Southern Baptist minister in 1939. He was educated in conservative Christian colleges: Bob Jones University of Greenville, South Carolina, the Florida Bible Institute (now called Trinity College) near Tampa, and Wheaton College in Illinois, where he received a bachelor of arts degree in anthropology in 1943.

On August 13, 1943, he married Ruth McCue Bell, a fellow student and daughter of a medical missionary. Their first daughter, Virginia, was born two years later, followed by Anne in 1948, Ruth in 1950, and sons William in 1952 and Nelson in 1958. For many years, the Graham family made its home in Montreat, North Carolina.

After a period as minister of the First Baptist Church in Western Springs, Illinois, Graham became a traveling "tent evangelist," a calling which, in a few years, brought him to national prominence. He met singer George Beverly Shea, and song leader Cliff Barrows, and the three formed a lasting partnership. Their revival meetings in small churches developed a following. In 1949, Graham, Shea and Barrows had a meeting in Los Angeles. Rather than their usual crowd of 3,000 or so, more than 10,000 turned out to hear this backwoods preacher and his team.

Graham launched his worldwide ministry with his first overseas tour in 1954 to Great Britain. Crowds of more than two million people attended his rallies. He even met with Queen Elizabeth II. At a 16-week rally in New York City three years later, more than two million packed Madison Square Gardens to hear the young preacher. Graham has preached before an estimated 210 million people in 185 countries—more than any other person in history.

Dr. Graham's message has remained the same and is based on traditional Biblical study. It is simply this: "Choose Christ as I did. Mankind is sinful, but through Christ, those sins are forgiven and people can live in peace." In other words, this is a message of love and hope.

Graham has been friends with many world figures, especially U.S. presidents, starting with Harry Truman who sought advice from Graham, and Richard Nixon, who was a frequent golf partner. On April 9, 1996, together with President William Clinton, Graham led 12,000 mourners in Oklahoma City to grieve for victims of the Federal Building bombing. He has been the chaplain at many Presidential Inaugural ceremonies; in fact, his 80th Inauguration invocation in January 1997, was inspired by our founding fathers, noting that "technology and social engineering had yet to solve the ancient problems of human greed and selfishness."

Graham, in his 80's, is slowing down because of his advancing illness, Parkinson's disease. The disease will eventually take away his ability to feed himself or even button his clothes. He walks with difficulty now and can hardly write his name. Ruth, his wife, never slows down. Her presence and vitality help ease the frustration brought on by his illness.

Dr. Graham's crusades have taken him to all the major cities in the United States, Europe and to such far-off areas as North Africa, India and Australia. Although a fundamentalist in his theology, individualistic in his religious and ethical approach, and traditional in his appeal, he always sought and obtained a broad base of ecumenical support for his evangelistic campaigns. Graham brought evangelism to a new level of sophistication in organization, technique, support and prestige. He once stated that "It seems to me that the whole world, regardless of culture and religious tradition, is searching for something spiritual. The most important thing that counts is what happens in the hearts of men." Billy Graham is the most respectable symbol of American evangelicalism.[1]

> *When wealth is lost, nothing is lost; when health is lost, something is lost; when character is lost, all is lost.*
>
> —Billy Graham

Christopher Reeve's Courageous Steps

From his first appearance at the Williamstown Theatre Festival at the age of 15, Christopher Reeve established a reputation as one of our country's leading actors. However, when he was paralyzed in an equestrian competition in 1995, Reeve not only put a human face on spinal-cord injury, but he motivated neuroscientists around the world to overcome the most complex diseases of the brain and central nervous system. After a surgery to fuse the neck vertebrae he shattered, Reeve could be elevated to a sitting position. With the exception of some movement in his shoulders, he remained paralyzed and unable to breathe without a respirator.

By the time he died, Christopher Reeve had at last "escaped the cape." He had become bigger than the Superman character he portrayed on the movie screen. Reeve championed cutting-edge research on spinal cord injury, offering himself as a guinea pig for new therapies and vowing he would one day walk again. He never did. However, his dream is now a plausible one for thousands of others who are paralyzed.

In 1999, Reeve became chairman of the Board of the Christopher Reeve Paralysis Foundation (CRPF)—a national, nonprofit organization that supports research to develop effective treatments and a cure for paralysis caused by spinal cord injury and other central nervous system disorders. CRPF also allocates a portion of its resources to grants that improve the quality of life for people with disabilities.

His second book, *Nothing is Impossible: Reflections on a New Life*, was published by Random House in September 2002. The audio version of *Nothing is Impossible* earned Reeve his second Grammy nomination for Best Spoken Word Album. At the same time, a documentary film, *Christopher Reeve: Courageous Steps*, telling of his advocacy and road to recovery, aired on ABC television. This documentary was directed by Reeve's son, Matthew, and has been distributed around the world.

In August 2004, Reeve completed directing his last project, *The Brooke Ellison Story*. This fact-based A&E cable television movie, which aired October 25, 2004, is based on the book, *Miracles Happen: One Mother, One Daughter, One Journey*. Brooke Ellison became a quadriplegic at age 11, but with the determination and the support of her family, Ellison rose above her disability and went on to graduate from Harvard University.

Reeve endured years of therapy to allow him to breathe for longer periods without a respirator, while tenaciously seeking a cure that would allow him to walk again. Reeve died October 10, 2004, after developing a serious bloodstream infection from a bedsore, a common problem for paralyzed people. He was 52 years old.

> *I refuse to allow a disability to determine how I live my life. I don't mean to be reckless, but setting a goal that seems a bit daunting actually is very helpful toward recovery.*
>
> —Christopher Reeve

Sherry's Ministry

Another person whom I consider a hero is a lady I will call Sherry. I first met her in a hospital room following a visit request by friends of the family. She was severely jaundiced and recovering from abdominal surgery that had revealed pancreatic cancer. Although in pain from her surgery, Sherry expressed her love for Christ and for sharing the Word at her home meetings.

Sherry was a member of a group seeking a new church in their town, approximately 25 miles from my home. Members of the group asked me for help in starting a church. I remembered Sherry had expressed a love for home meetings. With both thoughts in mind, I visited Sherry at her home after she was discharged from the hospital. No longer jaundiced, she was grateful that I had traveled such a distance just to see her. Even though she had a negative prognosis regarding her cancer, I sensed in her a need to continue in ministry. She was not ready to lie down and wait for death; she needed to be used by God.

Though in good spirits, Sherry was ill and would have difficult days ahead unless the Lord healed her. Yet, by her glowing countenance, I was prompted to ask if she would be willing to have home meetings again. We could start a church right there in her living room. She was delighted that I asked her, and she organized a meeting the next week. As I drove home, I realized how audacious it was of me to assume that a very ill woman should take on such a project. Once again, I was to realize that the grace of God would always supply His need.

Within a few short weeks, Sherry's home filled to overflowing with people desiring to worship together. She needed a bigger meeting place, and another member of their group had a perfect setting at his home. Sherry continued to lead the group in worship and study of the Word until the cancer began to take its toll on her strength.

Soon, she was back in the hospital nearing death. I visited her every day. One evening after I had left her room, her husband and daughter remained. Even though Sherry had fallen into a coma the day before, her daughter began to sing a chorus at the foot of her bed. Sherry sat up, looking at another unseen person in her room. Then she turned to kiss her husband and hugged her daughter and said "I love you." She laid her head back on the pillow and closed her eyes in death. I heard there was such a presence of the Lord in her room that praise came in place of tears. Those came later.

❝ *The biggest disease today is not leprosy or tuberculosis, but rather the feeling of being unwanted.* ❞

—Mother Teresa

Mother Teresa's Perseverance

In 1948, Mother Teresa stepped from the convent where she had taught for many years onto the streets of Calcutta, India, the first of the Missionaries of Charity. She had vowed to help the poorest of the poor. She was very poor herself and often had to beg. Begging was difficult. One priest must have thought she disgraced the church, as he had bristled when she asked him for money. His eyes narrowed in that deep disgust reserved for beggars. His voice snarled revulsion. His hands knotted into angry fists. After that day, she could not walk down that street where the priest had repulsed her without feeling a bitter sting.

However, Mother Teresa had greater challenges—help the poorest of the poor. On December 21, she rounded up five slum urchins by a mud hole to begin a school. She also had to attract 10 recruits to her new order within one year. The Archbishop had asked her to keep a journal. Her first entries were spirited: "I believe some are saying what (is the) use of working among this lowest of the low . . . (but) surely the lowest of the low can have the love and devotion of us few, 'the Slum Sister' they call me, and I am glad to be just that for His love and glory . . ."

However, progress was very slow and she attracted no recruits: "I am afraid . . . our Lord just wants me to be a 'Free Nun', covered with the poverty of the Cross. But today I learned a good lesson, the poverty of the poor must be often so hard for them. When I went around looking for a home, I walked and walked till my legs and arms ached. I thought how they must also ache in body and soul looking for home, food and help. Then the temptation grew strong. The palace buildings of Loreto came rushing into my mind. All the beautiful things and comforts; in a word, *everything*. 'You have only to say the word and all that will be yours again,' the tempter kept on saying . . . This is the dark night of the birth of the Society. My God, give me courage now, this moment, to persevere in following Your Will."

After many weeks, she had not attracted one novice. Failure loomed. "Today, my God, what tortures of loneliness. I wonder how long my heart will suffer this. Tears rolled and rolled. Everyone sees my weakness . . ."

She knew the saints, not that she was a saint, suffered many failures. No one escaped suffering or death. Would her tiny infant of an order die so soon?

Later, Mother Teresa would take the fisted hand of a novice involved in some very unpleasant duty and she would unfold the fingers one by one to the words of Jesus: You-do-this-for-Me![2]

Not all my heroes have been famous to the world, but some have. What has distinguished them has been their perseverance in spite of non-acceptance, suffering, poverty and illness. Each has left his or her mark on people's hearts.

> *So never lose an opportunity of urging a practical beginning, however small, for it is wonderful how often in such matters the mustard-seed germinates and roots itself.*
>
> —Florence Nightingale

Endnotes

[1] "William Franklin Graham, Jr." *Encyclopedia of World Biography*, 2nd ed. 17 Vols. Gale Research, 1998.

[2] Excerpts from Web pages, author: Chawla, Navin, *Mother Teresa*. UK: Sinclair-Stevenson, 1992.

Reflections for Discussion

1. How would you define the author's view of the word *hero* as it was used in this chapter?

2. Which heroes mentioned do you admire, and what made them heroes?

3. Do we as a people see others through Christ's eyes?

4. Rather than going in person to help, we prefer to send money. Do you agree?

5. List two or three of your personal heroes and discuss their contributions.

TWELVE

I Am Not a Loser

Can a person truly be productive in spite of pain and disability?

Just because I live in pain doesn't mean I am a member of the second team. I am as able as ever to speak and write. Granted, I cannot stand behind a pulpit, although I can use a stool for support to relieve my discomfort. My pain has not depleted my cognitive or creative abilities. Those who have relegated me to the bench are those who have doubts regarding my health and my ability to fulfill a job description. Their greatest concern is my impact on their health insurance plan.

I understand their feelings because I have been a company executive in charge of personal and insurance benefits. People and machinery have

> "Why should the righteous suffer?"
> "Why not?" replied Lewis. "They're the only ones who can handle it."
>
> —C.S. Lewis

something in common in the business world. A competent purchasing agent does not buy machinery that is second-rate and prone to breakdowns and constant repairs. A human resources manager views potential employees in a similar vein. They are looking for long-term dependability and the lowest-possible-cost employee for each job description.

Recognizing this, I have readjusted my priorities and career goals. Though I am as knowledgeable and productive as I was before my disability, I have made adjustments that allow my needs of self-worth and esteem to be fulfilled.

Earlier I mentioned Joni Eareckson Tada. She is an excellent example of one who has realigned her life from the tragedy of paralysis to become both productive and a source of encouragement. Not only is she an accomplished artist, but she is also an author, radio broadcaster, Web site owner, renowned speaker, and the list goes on.

66 *Most folks are about as happy as they make up their minds to be.* 99

—Abraham Lincoln

At first, a debilitating injury or illness may feel like a failure. However, for a person who believes God, failure is not fatal. The grace of God meets us at our point of failure. "Do not rejoice over me, my enemy; when I fall, I will arise; when I sit in darkness, the Lord will be a light to me" (Micah 7:8).

Normal Christian experience includes reversals of lifestyle through everyday circumstances. We are not immune from accidents, wars and disease. The Greek word for *suffering* in Romans 5:2-5 *NIV* means "pressure, distress of the mind and circumstances, trial and affliction." The wonder of it all is that God chooses to shine through us to show His power.

How does God see us?

Circumstances of life may appear on the surface to be distressful and not for our good. God does not look at us as failures because we lack success or strength and have poor health. He looks at our hearts. I am convinced that God is more concerned with the way I handle my relationships and myself during trials. I think of Joseph who was cast into a pit, sold into slavery by his brothers, and innocently imprisoned. Yet, after the death of his father, he spoke these words to his brothers. "But as for you, you meant evil against me; but God meant it for good, in order to bring it about as it is this day, to save many people alive" (Genesis 50:20).

I have loved this next Scripture because of the use of simile (unlike things are compared). Paul speaks of a treasure in earthen vessels. It was common in his day for thieves to enter into homes and steal everything of value. To keep their valuables safe, a family would place them in common earthen vessels rather than decorative or glazed ones. They might even bury their vessel in the earth floor of their home. Thieves would overlook a common vessel and steal the more attractive one when in reality the riches were in common earthen vessels. Paul, being aware of this practice, uses the illustration to compare our bodies to earthen vessels. It is not beauty, "six-pack abs" or large biceps that show the power of God. The common, everyday person with his frailities shows God's power. "But we have this treasure in earthen vessels, that the excellence of the power may be of God and not of us" (2 Corinthians 4:7).

Can God's power be visible in weak people?

The apostle Paul could not get rid of a troublesome personal weakness he called his *thorn*. It undermined his self-confidence and kept him from being the strong leader people expected. Three times he prayed concerning it, but his prayers did not change his weakness. As he nursed his stinging disappointment, he heard God say,

> "My grace is sufficient for you, for My strength is made perfect in weakness. Therefore most gladly I will rather boast in my infirmities, that the power of Christ may rest upon me" (12:9).

It gave him a new perspective on failure. If God could demonstrate His strength through human weakness, then Paul, instead of feeling embarrassed, would make his failure a focus of rejoicing and hope.

> ❝ When I was a young man I observed that nine out of ten things I did were failures. I didn't want to be a failure, so I did ten times more work. ❞
>
> —George Bernard Shaw

We need to have a dream if we are going to make a dream come true. A dream of a better life with meaning and importance is not limited by physical deformities or disabilities. A dream is limitless with unrealized opportunities. This little saying describes it well: "It doesn't do any good to sit up and take notice if you keep on sitting." Your dream requires action in order to reach fulfillment; otherwise, it is merely a daydream.

The most depressed and discouraged people are those who do not see a future that is better than the present. Those who are content to sit in their misery will soon find themselves alone. Dreamers who just dream and tell great stories of "What will be" will lose their validity unless they do something productive.

> *If you really want to do something, you will find a way. If you don't, you will find an excuse.*
>
> —Anonymous

What are your top three priorities in life? Take time to list them. Whether they are financial, relational or spiritual, be realistic by making them reachable. Priorities need to be measurable to notice a difference in your life when a certain point of your goal is reached. These milestones, or points of achievement, should be accomplished within a set period of time. Do not set a priority in the "sweet by and by." Rather, give it six months or a year. Then during that time, check your progress to make sure you are going forward and not stopped at the beginning or faltered in the middle.

Here are some steps to overcoming the law of inertia.

- Get off your bench and set a path and a route to where you want to be.
- Develop an intense desire to reach your goal so you know with absolute certainty that you will never ever give up.

- Have an unstoppable belief in yourself and eliminate fear and doubt forever.

> *No one can make you feel inferior without your consent.*
>
> —Eleanor Roosevelt

Anxiety and fear will strip away courage and make great performances impossible. Doubt makes even your best decisions seem difficult and causes procrastination. Anger tears your focus away from your goals. Frustration can provide a way to make you quit. Guilt makes it impossible to enjoy any successes you achieve. In reading this, did you notice that the things that can actually stop you are your own thoughts and emotions?

During a meeting with some other pastors, one pastor mentioned the Scripture, "I can do all things through Christ which strengtheneth me" (Philippians 4:13, KJV). He was having difficulty with the word *which*. He did not think "which" was an appropriate word to use with Christ. He mentioned the Lord's Prayer as it begins, "Our Father which art in heaven." He then said that to him the Scripture means he can do all things through Christ, and the knowledge of that fact, strengthens him. In other translations the word, *which* is translated "who." Theologically, he was mistaken, but logically, his interpretation has had a lasting effect upon me. I liked the thought that I can do all things through Christ and knowing that, I am strengthened. I also live by the Scripture when it reads, "I can do all things through Christ *who* strengthens me" (emphasis added).

When you set a goal or plan your dream, you need to write down a list of potential obstacles you may face.

- Are there people who will not understand your goal and discourage you?
- Do physical limitations or unfavorable circumstances stand in your way?
- If there are perceived barriers, how are you going to overcome them?

List them, *analyze* them and develop a *plan*. With a roadblock, you can turn off before you get there or go over, under and around it by following your plan. Do the same with obstacles that seem to make it impossible for you to reach goals. Is there a way you can bypass the objects of resistance you are going to face? When you reach an obstacle, you know what to do. You already have a contingency plan, so move ahead and reach the goals you have set!

What about asking for assistance?

It is important to identify the people or organizations that can help you reach your goals. Research the subject of goal setting and talk to people who have accomplished the same goals you are seeking. Get their input by asking how they did it and how they felt when they reached their goals.

This is what I had to do. I have written articles and papers, but I did not know where to start with a book. The first thing I did was try to find books similar to what I wanted to present. I searched the Web for ideas and found a source that explained a simple process. I am turning my dream into reality; I am changing my sense of worth and esteem. I just needed to do the research and get started.

> *Most of us know perfectly well what we ought to do; our trouble is that we do not want to do it.*
>
> —Peter Marshall

The following article tells of a person faced with the ultimate trial. Yet he refused to be a loser on or off the court.

U.S. tennis champion Arthur Ashe underwent heart-bypass surgery in 1983. At that time, hospitals were not checking blood samples for H.I.V. (the virus that causes AIDS). Through a blood transfusion, Ashe contracted the dreaded disease. He did not suspect that he was infected until 1988, when he had to have brain surgery after his right arm became paralyzed. Surgery revealed a parasitic infection that led to a diagnosis of AIDS. Ashe had not planned to reveal his illness until the time came when the disease would noticeably change him physically. However, *USA TODAY* demanded he confirm or deny the rumor that he had AIDS in 1992. The tennis star, ranked seventh in the world before forced to retire, bravely held a press conference and announced that he was indeed an AIDS victim.

Like anyone else, Arthur Ashe was tempted to aim his rage at God, but he conquered that temptation. Speaking at the Niagara County Community College in the fall of 1992, he testified to the place Jesus Christ held in his life.

"I've had a religious faith, growing up in the South and black and having the church as a focal point of my life," Ashe said. "And I was reminded of something Jesus said on the cross: 'My God, my God, why hast thou forsaken me?'

Remember, Jesus was poor, humble and of a despised minority. I wasn't poor in that my father was a policeman, but we certainly weren't rich. And Jesus asked the question, in effect, of why must the innocent suffer. And I'm not so innocent—I mean, I'm hardly a perfect human being—but you ask about yourself, 'Why me?' And I think, Why not me?"

"Why should I be spared what some others have been inflicted with," he continued. "And I have to think of all the good of my life, of having a great wife and daughter, and family and friends, and winning Wimbledon and the U.S. Open and playing for and coaching the Davis Cup team, and getting a free scholarship to U.C.L.A.—all kinds of good things. You could also ask about this, 'Why me?' Sometimes there are no explanations for things, especially for the bad." [1]

> *The Winner is always part of the answer.*
> *The Loser is always part of the problem.*
> *The Winner always has a program.*
> *The Loser always has an excuse.*
> *The Winner says, "Let me do it for you."*
> *The Loser says, "That's not my job."*
> *The Winner sees an answer for every problem.*
> *The Loser sees a problem for every answer.*
> *The Winner sees a green near every sand trap*
> *The Loser sees two or three sand traps near every green.*
> *The Winner says, "It may be difficult but it's possible."*
> *The Loser says, "It might be possible but it's too difficult."*
> *Be a Winner.*

—Vince Lombardi

Endnote

[1] Dr. William P. Barker, *TARBELL'S TEACHER'S GUIDE*, (Elgin, Illinois: David C. Cook Church Ministries, 1994).

Reflections for Discussion

1. Do you agree that God is more concerned with the way people handle their relationships and themselves during trials?

2. What is the great treasure that is hidden within our earthen vessels?

3. Do you think it is important to have prioritized goals at all of life's stages?

4. What is the first obstacle to overcome if you are to move forward?

5. Vince Lombardi's quotation is full of wisdom and understanding. Take some time to reflect upon it.

THIRTEEN

Becoming a Better Person Through Suffering

Jesus promised His disciples three things: that they would be entirely fearless, absurdly happy, and that they would get into trouble.

—W. Russell Maltby

Can anything good come from suffering?

After reading this chapter title, I can already hear voices saying, "Is he kidding?" "What is there about this disfigured body that makes me a better person?" "I am confined to a bed, what is so wonderful about that?" "I am just 15 years old, and I can't walk." "What is going to make me a better person?"

When Jesus promised His disciples that they would suffer trial and tribulations, He did not mean they would have mild setbacks. Just one of His disciples lived and died at an old age; however, he was boiled in oil during the persecutions in Rome. Can you imagine the scarring from his burns that may have hampered John's movement or disfigured his hands? In spite of his torture, trials and exile, John wrote the Book of Revelation and three letters.

Joseph's Difficulties

Another Biblical figure who exemplifies a dedicated man of God in spite of his dire circumstances is Joseph. Disdained by his brothers, sold into slavery and placed in prison under false accusations are hardly the types of situations we would like to find ourselves in. Most know the end of the story. Joseph became governor of Egypt and saved his family from famine. His told his brothers that, though they had sold him into slavery, it had turned out for the good of his family. We can read this story in the Book of Genesis, chapters 37 through 47, in less than a half hour, but we must remember that many years pass. Joseph was 17 at the start of the story, and by the time he was governor of Egypt, he was a grown man. When I read stories of Joseph and Paul the apostle, I try to picture the period and circumstances surrounding them to appreciate the fortitude and dedication of these men. They did not give up at the first sign of difficulty, but they continued with purpose to serve God.

C.S. Lewis says it well, "God whispers in our pleasures but shouts in our pain. Pain is His megaphone to rouse a dulled world." If all of your life experience is peace and prosperity, you are poorly prepared for turmoil and poverty.

The lottery has become a billion-dollar business. Everyone wants to win the Publisher's Clearing House contest and become a millionaire. The reality is that you have a better chance of being hit by lightning in a coal mine than becoming rich through lotteries and contests. It is the story of winners that keeps people coming back and spending their hard-earned money rather than giving to a charity for cancer research or muscular dystrophy.

He Changed the World for the Blind

Louis was from a small town called *Coupvray*, near Paris. He was born on January 4, 1809. Louis became blind by accident when he was 3 years old. In his father's harness workshop, he tried to be like Dad, but a mishap changed his life. He grabbed an awl, a sharp tool for making holes; the tool slipped and injured his eye. His wound became infected, and the infection spread. Soon, Louis was blind in both eyes.

In school, he could not learn everything just by listening, but things appeared to improve when Louis received a scholarship to the Royal Institution for Blind Youth in Paris when he was 10. Even there, most of the teachers just talked to the students. The library had 14 huge books with raised letters that were difficult to read.

In 1821, a former soldier named Charles Barbier visited the school. Barbier shared his invention called "night writing," a code of 12 raised dots that allowed soldiers to share top-secret information on the battlefield without having to speak. Regrettably, the code was too difficult for the soldiers, but not for 12-year-old Louis.

Louis changed Barbier's 12 dots into six and perfected the system by the time he was 15. He published the first Braille book in 1829, but he did not stop there. In 1837, he added symbols for math and music. However, since the public was skeptical, blind students had to study Braille on their own. Even at the Royal Institution, where Louis taught after he graduated, Braille was not taught until after his death. Braille began to spread worldwide in 1868, when a group of British men, from what is now known as the Royal National Institute for the Blind, took up the cause. Today, most countries in the world use Braille. Pain and injury gave Louis Braille a purpose and the world of the blind changed forever.

> *Life is an onion. You peel it off one layer at a time, and sometimes you weep.*
>
> —Carl Sandburg

How does pain realistically make you a better person? For one thing, it gives you the ability to empathize. Instead of just saying, "I know how you feel," you truly *do* understand. Recently, someone told me of someone they knew who was worse off than I was. I agreed. Yes, there are others with more complex disabilities. However, the person who made the remark had never walked in my shoes or the shoes of the other person. I pointed out that it is common for people to come to those conclusions, but those types of remarks instill feelings of guilt or anger. When you find yourself being compared to another, be patient and kind with the one speaking. You will retain them as a friend rather than losing a great relationship.

Franklin D. Roosevelt was on his way up the political ladder of success when in the summer of 1921 he was crippled by polio at Campobello Island.

Alden Hatch says that "in a peculiar sense, the attack of polio was the best thing that ever happened" to the future president. It provided him time to do what had been long neglected: studying, learning and thinking. "Plus," Hatch says, it also "gave him compassion."

> *Many historians point to the social policies of Roosevelt as his greatest contributions to the country. Though rich, the compassion he learned in his fight with polio made him cognizant of the needs of others.*

—Alden Hatch

What is empathy?

Empathy is "the action of understanding, being aware of, being sensitive to, and vicariously experiencing the feelings, thoughts and experiences of another of either the past or present without having the feelings, thoughts, and experience fully communicated in an objectively explicit manner."[1] Compare this with the definition of *sympathy*: "an affinity, association, or relationship between persons or things wherein whatever affects one similarly affects the other."[2]

Empathy does not require the person who is suffering to explain all the small details, because the listener is already able to understand and be sensitive to their needs. Sympathy requires that both share the same experience. Sympathy shows when a person yawns. It will often cause another to yawn. A person who has empathy has an ability to reach many more people with real support than just sympathy.

"The power of the church is not a parade of flawless people, but of a flawless Christ who embraces our flaws. The church is not made up of the whole people, rather of the broken people who find wholeness in a Christ who was broken for us."[3] Never have I seen this statement better fulfilled than by a small group in our church. The members of the group were plain, everyday people with an extraordinary desire to minister. Granted, they were not perfect people, but their purpose was flawless.

A neighbor of one of the members had terminal cancer. He did not belong to our church, but that was not important. He was in need. He was bedridden, without a source of income and had a wife and children to support. The group graciously ministered to the man. Then they made certain that food and other necessities were available for his family. They painted his house and did other repairs his wife was unable to complete. When he died, their ministry did not. The group continued to care for the family until its members were able to recover and support themselves. The group's outreach changed the lives of all in the home, and Christ became part of a new family. Flawed people performed a flawless ministry.

Had it not been for his imprisonment, Paul would not have written the 14 epistles. Had it not been for the imprisonment of John Bunyan, he would not have authored *Pilgrim's Progress*. Had it not been for his fall from a horse, we would not have had Tolstoy's *War and Peace*. Had it not been for the early blindness that afflicted Helen Keller, she would not have been able to contribute so much to improve the plight of the blind. As previously noted, had it not been for the early blindness of Louis Braille, Braille would never have been invented.

What made these ordinary people extraordinary?

They could have wallowed in their distress. They could have cried out, "Why?" They could have become embittered. It was not their plight or disability, but it was their desire to turn their personal world around. When they changed themselves, they changed the lives of millions. I would much rather help than to be helpless. Wouldn't you?

> *Faith is taking the first step even when you don't see the whole staircase.*
>
> —Martin Luther King Jr.

"I am beginning to understand that faith is not the way around pain, it is the way through pain. Faith doesn't get rid of the opposition, it invites it over for dinner. Faith doesn't give you the winning point at the last second, it ties the game and sends you into overtime. Faith doesn't give you the solution, it forces you to find it." [4] This insight is divine.

> "Therefore we do not lose heart. Though outwardly we are wasting away, yet inwardly we are being renewed day by day. For our light and momentary troubles are achieving for us an eternal glory that far outweighs them all" (2 Corinthians 4:16, 17, *NIV*).

During my most painful episodes, no matter how often I have asked God to remove my pain, He has not given me relief. However, He has changed my attitude. I have not spoken an unkind word to those around me. I even made a promise to myself. After prior surgeries when regaining consciousness, I often heard other people groaning and moaning from pain. Prior to a very painful surgery, I decided to say something funny when I awoke in the recovery room. This time when I woke up, my pain was excruciating and I could say very little, but I did manage, "Did you get the number of the truck that hit me?" I immediately went into shock, but at least I had kept my promise, and it was nice to hear the nurses laugh. They were still giggling as they covered me with warm blankets and eased my pain.

We must never forget our caregiver.

I refer here to the mother, father, sibling or spouse who cares for the ill or disabled. Caregivers must have a time for rest and reprieve. Caregiving can result in giving out and falling ill. I believe that I have a comprehension of the stress and emotional pain that is involved. I cared for two dying parents at the same time, and my health suffered. I have mentioned this before, but I want to reiterate the importance of the caregivers caring for themselves as they do for their loved ones. When possible, they should take some time for themselves. They might ask someone to fill in for them while they regain strength and spirit. A caregiver must find balance between the needs of self and the needs of the ill person.

If you are the one who is ill or disabled, remember that the way you respond to those helping you will affect the quality of care you receive. Even professional caregivers appreciate a kind word and a thank you. Remember the old saying, "Your walk talks louder than your talk walks."

Let the light of Christ shine through you.

“ *Tragedy struck opera singer Beverly Sills when her first child was born almost totally deaf. This little child would never hear the beautiful voice of her mother or the lovely sounds of a soft forest. Shortly after discovering the deafness, Mrs. Sills gave birth to a second child, only to find that this son was mentally retarded.*

So great was the sorrow of her life that she took off a full year from her profession to work with her daughter and son, trying to come to terms with the double tragedy.

Later, when asked how she learned to cope, the famed songstress said, "The first question you ask is, Why me? Then it changes to Why them? It makes a complete difference in your attitude." ”

—C.R. Hembree

Endnotes

[1] *Merriam-Webster's Medical Dictionary*, © 2002 Merriam-Webster, Inc.

[2] *Merriam-Webster's Medical Dictionary*, © 2002 Merriam-Webster, Inc.

[3] Mike Yaconelli, excerpt from article at Web site: *http://www.youthspecialties.com/articles/Yaconelli/inept.php*

[4] Mike Yaconelli, excerpt from article at Web site: *http://www.youthspecialties.com/articles/Yaconelli/annoy.php*

Reflections for Discussion

1. Joseph spent many years in slavery and imprisonment, yet he never lost his sense of purpose. How well would you have handled similar circumstances of being rejected and forgotten?

2. What does it mean to empathize, and how is it different from sympathy?

3. Are you a caregiver or do you know a caregiver? What does a caregiver need?

4. What was Beverly Sills' response when asked how she was able to cope with her family situation?

5. How powerful is personal attitude during times of distress, pain and sorrow?

FOURTEEN

"Our feelings do not affect God's facts."

—Amy Carmichael

Acceptance Must Be in My Vocabulary!

Is acceptance an appropriate response for a Christian?

This chapter's subject has the potential to be as controversial as Chapter 2, "What You Cannot See." Why? Because the same attitude exists. If I accept my pain or illness, then I am confessing it and that is negative faith. Positive faith says that I should not accept my situation, but have the faith that heals. Now that I have lived in pain for 25 years, I believe it is time I accepted the fact that there is damage within my body, and I must get on with my life.

I was attending a Christian men's meeting when a young man was wheeled into the room. It was his first visit, and I could tell he was uncomfortable with all the attention he immediately received. The proceedings halted as one man stated that we should pray for our newcomer to get up and walk away from his wheel chair. That room was full of noise as some shouted at demons, others cried to the Lord and several spoke loudly in tongues.

Prayer continued for at least 15 minutes until slowly, one by one, prayer warriors returned to their seats. At last, our visitor was left alone—still in his wheel chair. Even though there were no verbal comments regarding the fact that the young man had not walked, I could sense a feeling of disappointment because we were not going to see a miracle. It also appeared that the young man wished he were somewhere else.

What went wrong? Did the men have enough faith? I believe that some of them did, as I had witnessed their prayer and faith in action before. Did the young man block God's will? I do not believe he would have refused a healing and the prospect of joyfully walking away from his wheel chair. Following the meeting, I heard others suggesting that he had accepted his condition and his acceptance of paralysis prevented God's healing power. I am always surprised at how fast people find a weakness in God's power or a person's faith, rather than accept a situation as God's will. One thing I am sure is that we offended and pushed him away from the fellowship because I never saw him again at our meetings.

Once again, I have opened another can of spiritual worms. I am told that it cannot be God's will for someone to be bound to a wheel chair, suffer pain or have a debilitating illness. We run into Job's problem when acceptance is translated into God's will. We still need an answer that will satisfy our human desire for an explanation. We need a starting and ending point and answers to our "why" when God has no beginning or end, and He does not always supply a simple answer. Some will say that God does have a beginning and end when Jesus uses the term *Alpha and Omega*, but that is His title, not a description. God always was and will be forevermore. We are not going to fully comprehend that immense concept. We are not always going to know the answers no matter how hard we ask or try to understand.

Was it God's will for Joni Eareckson Tada to break her neck in a diving accident?

Let's approach this question from another view. If I fall off a 10-story building, is it God's will for me to break my body and probably die? If I fall off a building onto a cement sidewalk, I am quite sure I will not get up and walk away. It now becomes a question of, not just distance and circumstance, but also personal will. Did I choose to jump or was my fall accidental? At 10 stories high, the outcome will be the same. I believe you are beginning to see our dilemma.

If Joni had not broken her neck, we would not have her beautiful paintings, her weekly broadcasts or more than 30 books with topics ranging from disability outreach to reaching out to God. Her courage as a quadriplegic is still a source of encouragement and strength to millions. Because of her best-selling books, beginning with her autobiography, *Joni*, as well as having visited 35 countries, Joni's first name is recognized around the world. World Wide Pictures' full-length feature film, *JONI*, in which Mrs. Tada recreated her own life, has been translated into 15 languages and shown in scores of countries around the world. Mrs. Tada is a highly sought-after conference speaker, both in the U.S. and internationally, and was also a columnist for *Moody Magazine*, the United Kingdom's *Christian Herald*, and several European Christian magazines. This is just a portion of her biography. You can read about her ministry on the Web at *www.joniandfriends.org/about/tadabio.shtml*.

The purpose of *Joni and Friends* is advocating a Biblical response toward disabilities, both visible and invisible; providing opportunities for disability awareness; educating the church community in practical ways of serving disabled persons; and assisting persons with disabilities in their progress toward independence and fulfillment. Their mission and vision statements are also available on the Web site.

My reason for reprinting the purpose of *Joni and Friends*, a non-profit organization, is to help visualize the concept of acceptance for the disabled and infirmed. I know that Joni has accepted her disability, and by acceptance, a great ministry exists today to serve our world.

Therefore we do not lose heart. Though outwardly we are wasting away, yet inwardly we are being renewed day by day. For our light and momentary troubles are achieving for us an eternal glory that far outweighs them all (2 Corinthians 4:16, 17, *NIV*).

What are some benefits of suffering?

Suffering presents an opportunity for people to grow in perseverance and maturity leading to wisdom and obedience to God.

"My brethren, count it all joy when you fall into various trials, knowing that the testing of your faith produces patience. But let patience have its perfect work, that you may be perfect and complete, lacking nothing. If any of you lacks wisdom, let him ask of God, who gives to all liberally and without reproach, and it will be given to him" (James 1:2-5).

In suffering and pain, we have an opportunity to develop the virtue of contentment, which is not dependent on our circumstances in life. We experience acceptance and victory over our ill feeling (Philippians 4:11, 12). In our illness or disability, we learn to trust and depend on God (2 Corinthians 12:9) and renew our appreciation of His faithfulness.

Often it is in our trials and sickness that we overcome our own self-centeredness, and we learn empathy to comfort others (2 Corinthians 1:3-5). Perhaps the greatest asset is that our illness reminds us of our human limitations. In our weakness and limitation, we encounter God as our Creator, Lord and Judge. At the same time, we are given a chance to experience a loving merciful Father, who gave us His Son as our healer.

There is no better example of one who learned to accept his circumstances than Jesus. In the Garden of prayer, He asked His Father not to let Him go through the upcoming torture and terrible death of the Cross. However, He submitted to His Father's will by casting aside His own.

Would modern man understand the situation if he witnessed the actual events? I think man would have the same difficulty as he does now. How can suffering be the will of a loving God? That is the proverbial question of a non-Christian or a nominal believer. When we see through God's perspective, we have an entirely different way to deal with our sickness and suffering. In fact, the real test of our commitment to a God-centered life is precisely in how we deal with suffering during our sickness.

> *God will not permit any troubles to come upon us, unless He has a specific plan by which great blessing can come out of the difficulty.*
>
> —Peter Marshall

When your time of recovery or acceptance results in feelings of anger, it is often because someone or something has blocked your goal and is preventing you from accomplishing what you wanted. How do you feel in a traffic jam when it is preventing you from getting to work on time? Does your impatience lead to anger?

Is God really in control?

When you feel anxious in sickness or recovery, your anxiety may be signaling that your view of the future is uncertain. You are hoping something will happen, but you have no guarantee it will. You can control some of the factors, but not all of them. That is not normal, because we want to be in control of our lives. The truth is that as believers, peace comes when we recognize that it is God who is in control.

When you base your future success on something that can never happen, you have an impossible, hopeless goal. Your depression is a signal that your goal, no matter how spiritual or noble, may never be reached. We can be depressed for biochemical reasons, but if there is no physical cause, then depression is often rooted in a sense of hopelessness and helplessness.

To live successful lives, we need to distinguish a godly goal from a human desire. This distinction can spell the difference between inner peace and inner distress for the Christian. A godly goal is any action that reflects God's purpose for your life. It is not dependent on people or circumstances beyond your ability or right to control. Who do you have the ability and right to control? Actually, no one but yourself. The one person who can block a godly goal or determine its certainty is you. If you adopt an attitude of cooperation with God's plan as Jesus and Paul did, your goal is reachable. It should be obvious by now that God's basic goal for your life is to become the person God wants you to be.

> *We who lived in the concentration camps can remember the men who walked through the huts comforting others, giving away their last piece of bread. They may have been few in number, but they offer sufficient proof that everything can be taken from a man but one thing: the last of his freedoms—to choose one's attitude in any given set of circumstances, to choose one's own way.*
>
> —Victor S. Frankl

God does well in giving us grace of consolation, but man does not return everything gratefully to God. How can the gifts of grace flow in us when we are ungrateful to the Giver? When we do not return them to God, we become self-centered. Grace is always given to those who are grateful. To those who are not, it will be given to the humble, not the proud.

I do not want anyone's pity. My desire is that God shine through my life, and that men respect my relationship with Him. My greatest desire is to live with a peaceful acceptance and to die with grace.

"Disappointments—His Appointment"

Change one letter, then I see
That the thwarting of my purpose
Is God's better choice for me.
His appointment must be blessing,
Tho' it may come in disguise,
For the end from the beginning
Open to His wisdom lies.
No good will He withhold,
From denials oft we gather
Treasures of His love untold.
Well He knows each broken purpose
Leads to fuller, deeper trust,
And the end of all His dealings
Proves our God is wise and just.
Lord, I take it, then, as such,
Like clay in the hands of a potter,
Yielding wholly to Thy touch.
My life's plan is Thy molding;

Not one single choice be mine;
Let me answer, unrepining—
"Father, not my will, but Thine."

—Author Unknown

❝ *We shall draw from the heart of suffering itself the means of inspiration and survival.* ❞

—Sir Winston Churchill

Reflections for Discussion

1. Is acceptance of an illness, disease or tragedy a lack of faith?

2. Was it God's will for Joni Eareckson Tada to break her neck in a diving accident?

3. Would she have had an impact on others if the accident never happened?

4. What is your reaction to delays in traffic, difficult airline flights, lost luggage or unexpected vehicle problems?

5. How does a person show his or her appreciation to God for the grace and gifts that He has bestowed?

FIFTEEN

Walking Faith

"*If you want to hear God's voice clearly and you are uncertain, then remain in His presence until He changes this uncertainty. Often much can happen during this waiting for the Lord. Sometimes He changes pride into humility; doubt into faith and peace. . . .*"

—Corrie ten Boom

What does it mean to walk by faith?

The first humans failed in their test of faith. They placed their trust in what they saw, rather than believing what God said. Adam and Eve became the first example of people choosing to walk by sight, rather than faith. God's words to them were explicit, but they chose another path. We have followed this example ever since. We prove that Adam and Eve's faithlessness was not just a Biblical event, but also a trait of every human. We know the consequences of their faithlessness. They were driven from the Garden of Eden, yet even worse, it destroyed the close relationship they had with God.

"For all people walk each in the name of his god, but we will walk in the name of the Lord our God forever and ever" (Micah 4:5).

We definitely serve a loving God. This Scripture from Micah declares that the people will walk in the name of God forever and ever. However, in chapter 7, Micah declares: "The faithful man has perished from the earth, and there is no one upright among men. They all lie in wait for blood; every man hunts his brother with a net" (v. 2).

A walk of faith has never been a consistent trait of humankind, nevertheless God continues to love us. Individuals have exhibited a walk of faith that pleased the Lord. Both Enoch and Elijah were allowed to bypass natural death and were taken up into heaven. It is possible to walk in faith and be pleasing to God, though very few will be as Enoch and Elijah. (I am mindful of the end times and the catching up of the saints. I do not know when that will happen.)

The just shall live by faith is both a statement of fact regarding the basics of Christianity and a command. It is not a difficult concept to understand. Paul clarified this concept in 2 Corinthians 5:7 "For we walk by faith, not by sight." I presented a definition of faith earlier; however, it is worth repeating: "Belief does not rest on logical proof or material evidence." [1] At the end of the definitions, *belief* is listed as a synonym. However, in the Bible and practical Christianity, the two are very different. Merely believing and living by faith are not the same. Faith is so much more than just a belief in God. Living by faith involves qualities that are better expressed in the word, *trust*. Living, or walking by faith, exhibits loyalty and faithfulness in a person's life by works of obedience to God's Word.

The Israelites saw great miracles as they were led from captivity. Our mind cannot comprehend the Nile turning to blood or a sea separating so that the people could walk on dry land. However, at each point of a minor difficulty, the Israelites would complain and threaten rebellion. Even today, there are scoffers and doubters who deny the wonderful works of God.

My Salvation Experience

My conversion involved several key people who never gave up on me. One was a local Baptist minister who would approach me at town meetings or come to my home. After my conversion, we became great friends.

I was asked to give a short testimony at a Christian businessman's breakfast. On the evening before the meeting, the president of the local group called to ask me if I could lengthen my testimony. Their main speaker had become ill and was hospitalized. I agreed, but I was going to need some moral support, because I had never spoken to a public gathering in that manner before. I gave my Baptist minister friend a telephone call and asked if he would attend the breakfast. He did, and he even brought an unbeliever with him.

After I spoke, there was a feeling within the room that was new to me. The president of the group called for a time of prayer, and people began coming to the front. People were singing, praying and kneeling at their chairs. My friend brought the unbeliever to the front and asked the local president to pray for him. The leader had an unusual spiritual gift. It would sound like he was saying, "Tut, tut, tut, tut" as he began. He started to speak and touched the unbeliever, who immediately fell to the floor. Then he touched the Baptist minister who also fell to the floor. I just stood there in wonderment.

I knew that my Baptist minister did not believe in tongues or that type of activity during a church service. Therefore, I was reluctant to ask him what happened that Saturday morning. Two weeks later, I gathered the courage to ask him. His explanation was, "All I know was that the president said 'Work your mighty works, Lord;' then I was on the floor." I told him that I did not hear any English words spoken, and he did not believe me until we called the local president for verification. He acknowledged that he never spoke in English prior to touching my friend.

I then remembered the Book of Acts and this scripture: "We hear them speaking in our own tongues the wonderful works of God" (Acts 2:11). A new knowledge of God was born that morning in my friend. It was a miracle for him.

Several years later, I visited his home after an unsuccessful surgery. I was in pain as he asked if he could pray for me. I readily agreed and was blessed to hear a new language emanating from my him. Now I had seen a miracle. He had received the gift of the Holy Spirit and had also accepted healing as described in 2 Corinthians 12:9, 10.

Are there people who would scoff and disbelieve what I just wrote? Yes, there are. I can report what I saw and heard. I walk in faith—not seeking miracles; I walk in faith expecting them. There is a great difference.

> *He who has faith has . . . an inward reservoir of courage, hope, confidence, calmness, and assuring trust that all will come out well—even though to the world it may appear to come out most badly.*
>
> —B.C. Forbes

Many Christians have firmly believed that God would heal loved ones when they prayed in faith. Some were convinced that they had confirmation from other believers or from other miracles. Therefore, they were genuinely dumbfounded when their loved one died. What they had believed with such certainty turned out not to be true. Their faith could not heal the person. God could heal, though He chose not to, despite their prayers, their faith, Christian love and Biblical promises.

When these disappointments happen, a setback occurs. If faith in the healing turned out to be a misunderstanding, what happened to the power of God? Was it also a mistake or misinterpretation? That is one of the pitfalls of the "word-faith" teaching. It ties faith in our Savior to faith in predefined or desired outcomes.

Did Jesus promise to heal every disease?

He did not heal Epaphroditus, at least not as fast as they wanted Him to (Philippians 2:27). Even in His earthly ministry, Jesus did not heal everyone (see John 5:3-9). Scripture mentions a multitude of people at the Pool of Bethesda, yet Jesus chose to heal a certain man who had been ill for 38 years.

There are many questions a person may have regarding faith and a walking faith.

- Why does faith seem so imperative in other people's lives and so inconsequential in our own?
- Why does the healing power of faith seem so powerful in sermons and books and powerless in everyday life?
- Is it always God's will to heal people who have faith in Christ?

Biblical evidence supports that He sometimes does and sometimes does not. Stephen and James were killed. Eventually, all the first Christians died of something. With the exception of John, all of the disciples were martyred. Thousands died during the persecutions of Nero, Domitian and many other leaders of Rome—including the notorious Diocletian. Persecution continued not only in Rome, but also in Persia and in Europe under the Goths and the Vandels.

A study of Fox's Book of Martyrs will enlighten many to the price that was paid for following Christ. Persecutions continue today for those who serve the Savior, Jesus. Yet, how many times did God save them out of danger before they died? Perhaps many times.

Jesus promised persecution, not freedom from pain and sorrow.

When Paul was beaten, stoned and imprisoned, he felt pain, even though Jesus had paid the penalty of all sin. Paul had great faith, but he also had many sufferings

(2 Corinthians 1:5; Philippians 3:10; 4:12). Although Jesus atoned for all sin, Christians still suffer despite their faith. Some Christians will suffer because of their faith.

> *As your faith is strengthened you will find that there is no longer the need to have a sense of control, that things will flow as they will, and that you will flow with them, to your great delight and benefit.*
>
> —Emmanuel Teney

Why do Christians interpret Scripture differently?

Scripture is clear that one of the ministries of the Holy Spirit is to reveal the meaning of the Word so that we may understand (1 Corinthians 2:13, 14). This being true, why do Christians differ in their understanding of certain Bible verses?

To answer this question, I will compare the Holy Spirit to a television transmitter. In the 1950's through most of the 1970's, reception of the TV signal required an antenna. A signal was transmitted perfectly, but there were all kinds of antennas in our homes. There were rabbit ears swathed in aluminum foil to tall outside antennas with an ability to change direction. Television receivers were of different makes, various states of efficiency and repair. Sometimes a good slap on the television set would improve the picture quality. (Often, I think that is what I personally need.) My point is that there are various antennas and receivers with differing reception of the signal.

Christians are somewhat similar. The Holy Spirit's "signal" is always perfect. However, because of varying circumstances (perhaps sin, an immature walk in the Spirit, great concern of their worldly affairs, or being blinded by the Enemy of our souls), Christians have various degrees of success in properly receiving the Spirit's truth.

Faith in God is a requirement for the Christian life. The author of Hebrews stated:

> "But without faith it is impossible to please Him, for he who comes to God must believe that He is, and that He is a rewarder of those who diligently seek Him" (11:6).

We must believe who God is, what He says and what He does. This is a faith that turns the key to the kingdom of God.

> ❝ *Do I think faith will be an important part of being a good president? Yes, I do.* ❞
>
> —George W. Bush

Faith is the most important part of your Christian life. You are saved by faith (see Ephesians. 2:8, 9), and you "walk by faith, not by sight" (2 Corinthians. 5:7). In other words, faith is the basis for our salvation and the means by which we live. If we are going to live a life of freedom in Christ, it is important to remember these facts concerning faith. Belief or trust, belief in, devotion to, or trust in somebody or something, especially without logical proof, is a description of faith.

Faith depends upon a definite object. People throughout the world live by faith. The difference between Christian faith and non-Christian faith is the object of our faith. The differentiating factor is what and who you believe in. You cannot have faith in faith. Faith without a central focus becomes invalid. People cannot live by faith if they have no understanding of the object of their faith.

What would cause faith to falter?

The amount of faith you possess depends upon how well you know the object of your faith. A strong person of faith has a deep and unswerving understanding of God. If a person struggles with faith, it is not because God has failed. Instead, he or she has an incomplete knowledge of God. Unknowingly, people put restraints on God because of their own humanity. They attempt to relate to Him in a natural rather than spiritual way. If God fails to answer or respond in a certain way, a few will give up on Him.

To increase your faith, it is necessary to increase your knowledge of God. You will receive a proper return on your investment with God. If you do not know Him or His Word, you will have little faith. If you do know Him and His Word, you have potential for great faith. No other person can pump up your faith. Others may lift your feelings, but it is the Holy Spirit who teaches and empowers you.

> "And straightway the father of the child cried out, and said with tears, Lord, I believe; help thou mine unbelief" (Mark 9:24, KJV).

The following comment by Matthew Henry gives all a good comprehension of belief and faith.

> Those that complain of unbelief, must look up to Christ for grace to help them against it, and his grace shall be sufficient for them. "Help mine unbelief, help me to a pardon for it, help me with power against it; help out what is wanting in my faith with thy grace, the strength of which is perfected in our weakness."
>
> —Matthew Henry Unabridged

Faith depicts action because it requires results to be visible. James best describes this quality.

> "Thus also faith by itself, if it does not have works, is dead. But someone will say, 'You have faith, and I have works.' Show me your faith without your works, and I will show you my faith by my works" (James 2:17, 18)

A sure faith will affect your walk and your talk. James says that they must be the same. If we believe God and His Word and live by it, then everything we do will be a result of what we have chosen to believe.

In summary, faith depends on an object—God. The strength of faith will be a direct result of the depth of knowledge of God and His Word. The walk of faith will produce works, which in turn proves faith.

An evangelist was preaching on the Holy Spirit at our church. He said, "Do you want to see how to walk in the Spirit?" I was filled with anticipation thinking he had a great new revelation. He said, "I will show you." Then he walked back and forth across the speaking platform. There was nothing special in his walk or his method of walking. His point was that we walk in the Spirit when we have His knowledge and put it to work in our lives. This is what I call a "walking faith."

> *All I have seen teaches me to trust the Creator for all I have not seen.*
>
> —Ralph Waldo Emerson

Endnote

[1] *The American Heritage® Dictionary of the English Language*, Fourth Edition Copyright © 2000 by Houghton Mifflin Company.

Reflections for Discussion

1. Is it natural for a person to walk by sight rather than by faith?

2. What is the difference between belief and faith?

3. What happens when a person believes that he or she has heard from God, either personally or through another's confirmation, and the final answer is opposite or negative of what they expected?

4. Respond to the statement, "You cannot have faith in faith."

5. What does faith depend on, and how is it strengthened?

SIXTEEN

How Do I Affect Those Around Me?

"God's people may groan, but they may not grumble."

—Charles Haddon Spurgeon

What about the caregivers?

I have already mentioned the importance of the caregiver caring for themselves. The amount of time a caregiver will allot for his or her needs will depend upon the person under care. If you require care, do you allow your caregiver to take some personal time? Do you allow them to travel great distances to visit or vacation?

You may not realize that limitations are in place. Your caregiver will assume and adopt a lifestyle around your needs that may be of great comfort for you. However, it could lead to "burn out" for them. Because of the love your caregiver has for you, he or she will be subjected voluntarily to a life centered around your needs. I have observed this situation in several homes. If I were to ask caregivers if they felt hemmed in or limited, they would say no. It may be obvious to another family member or close friend but never between caregivers and their loved one.

I have mentioned my constant pain. However, other health factors in my life are cause for watchfulness. I observe my wife who is my caregiver, and I look for signs of fatigue, frustration and the fenced-in feeling. Because I love her, I have made a conscious effort to give her a life outside of my own. She traveled to Italy with her sister to visit my son and his wife. She goes to Bible study, attends a ladies organization know as "Red Hat" and travels home to visit her mother and relatives. There are friends who help me when she is away. One dear lady will clean our house or run errands, while another cooks some special meals. Our neighbors keep a watch on my movements to make sure I am all right. We have found ways for her to feel free, even though she cares for me.

Do you have an attitude of gratitude?

As a man, I have taken one large step in that direction. I have learned to watch her television shows! Every time she hands me something, I say, "Thank you." I tell her of my love for her. I order presents or flowers over the Internet for her. I am sure there is more that I can do, but I continually try to be aware of her needs and not just my own. I am aware of my male tendency toward selfishness. (I can hear the ladies saying, "Amen.") I pray that I will be pleasant to her and that she will never resent me because of my personal needs.

Another quick attitude check is, "Do I complain too often or too much?" Thank God, not for your problems, but for the strength he is building in you through the difficult experiences of your life. You can be sure God's perfect love will see you through. Complaints do not make situations better, rather they cause resentment or anger. People appreciate a smile and a kind word.

I had to take care of my elderly stepfather while my mother was in the hospital. Each morning I would bring his washing items, breakfast and toothbrush into his bedroom. My mother had it down to a system, while I was working from a list. I brought him all that was on the list but forgot his toothpaste. He never said a word and brushed his teeth without paste. I would have never known that I had left it out. A year later, I returned to my homestead for a visit and my cousin was commenting on my stepfather's care. She laughingly asked if I remembered the last time I had been home caring for my stepfather. I replied that I did and she told me of the forgotten toothpaste. My stepfather never said a word to me, but jokingly told my mother and cousin. The next time I had to care for him, I never forgot his toothpaste. I was not offended that he told someone else, I was grateful that he appreciated what I was doing for him without a word of criticism.

I am aware that a person's response to their caregiver will be somewhat dependent upon their lifestyle prior to illness or injury. If one is used to having all they desired, they may have difficulty accepting new or different services. Your meal portions may not be the same or the choice of dessert may not be your favorite. Your schedule must adjust to others as you become dependent. The loss of independence is difficult for anyone to accept. For some, they may never fully accept their condition, and their attitude will clearly show. Thankfully, most of those requiring care are grateful for those around them and the small things are graciously overlooked.

Am I critical of others?

Do I have a tendency to correct others when I believe they are wrong? Both of these questions should be answered with a resounding, "No!" Unfortunately, this is not always the case. I have heard people complain of their doctors, nurses, food and whatever else did not meet their supposed standards. If a person is truly living a life in Christ, these criticisms will not be heard. Paul says it very well in this scripture:

> "I am not saying this because I am in need, for I have learned to be content whatever the circumstances" (Philippians 4:11, *NIV*).

The many desperate situations Paul encountered would probably get the best of us. Yet he never appeared down-in-the-mouth, but he gave thanks in all things because it was God's will in Christ Jesus. "Be joyful always; pray continually; give thanks in all circumstances, for this is God's will for you in Christ Jesus" (1 Thessalonians 5:16-18, *NIV*).

There should never be "dry spells" in the Christian life. God said He would be like an artesian well in the life of a believer. Artesian wells bubble forth with a cold, fresh, endless supply of water from deep in the earth, quenching any thirst and always satisfying. This is a wonderful picture of the spiritual refreshment that belongs to the Spirit-filled person.

At a special luncheon many years ago, I had the privilege of sitting next to David du Plessis, also known as "Mr. Pentecost." After some chorus singing, he commented to me that what we had just sung was not Scriptural. The chorus was called "Fill My Cup." He continued by saying a Christian's cup should never need to be filled. It should be full all of the time. I understood what he meant, and looked forward to the day when I would feel full. Today I am a more mature Christian and no longer base my faith on feelings. Scripture tells me that I am full, though I may not feel it. I am so glad my relationship with God does not depend on my feelings.

Have you ever heard people say they are experiencing a dry spell in their Christian life? What are they saying? Are they saying that God ran out of water? As Mr. Pentecost said, "You should never run dry." You do not need to chase all over the country trying to find sources of spiritual refreshment. Conferences, retreats, books and tapes can all bring encouragement, but if you are a Christian, the source of living water already resides within you.

Why would you exchange an artesian well for a broken water tank? (Jeremiah 2:13) Artesian wells do not dry up; cracked cisterns do. If you are experiencing spiritual dryness right now, is it because you have been attempting to find your source of spiritual refreshment from man-made sources, which will fail you every time? Jesus extended an invitation to you when He said, "Whoever believes in me, as the Scripture has said, streams of living water will flow from within him" (John 7:38, *NIV*).

If you are being cared for and are unable to attend church or watch services on television, remind yourself of who you are in Christ. You are His, and He will never let you go. Do not drift too far from Him. Speak to the Lord and address the Holy Spirit in the first person. Talk to the Holy Spirit, and I am sure you will feel His presence during your special time of need.

Am I thankful for what I have?

If you are reading this book, then you already have more than most of the people in the world. Either you have received it as a gift from someone who cares for you or you could afford to purchase something other than the staple needs of life. I am thankful for the roof over my head and the warmth of love that makes a home. I am thankful that I can still walk some, that I am not bedridden, and that I am loved. Your list will be different from mine, but if you search within, I know that you will find a multitude of things for which you are thankful.

Do I want others to go through the same problems I have? My answer to that is no, but sometimes I wish they could walk in my shoes for a couple of minutes. Then they would understand and not criticize or mock me. No matter what illness or injury has occurred in our lives, we have no right wishing others would suffer the same. I would never want my children to endure the 26 surgeries and the pain I have experienced. If all people are God's children, then we already know He does not want us to suffer. That was His plan for His Son. Jesus suffered and died so that we may have forgiveness of sin and eternal life. God does not require us to suffer for salvation; that is finished.

Some will suffer for God. Missionaries and Christians living throughout the world have suffered and died for the faith. That suffering is something that Jesus told us to expect. Our physical suffering and sickness is a result of our humanity and man's choice not to obey God and His Word.

> "No discipline seems pleasant at the time, but painful. Later on, however, it produces a harvest of righteousness and peace for those who have been trained by it" (Hebrews 12:11, *NIV*).

In 1871, the famous Chicago fire ravaged the city. When it was all over, 300 people were dead and 100,000 were homeless.

Horatio Gates Spafford was one of many who tried to help the people of Chicago get back on their feet. As a lawyer, he had invested much of his money into the downtown Chicago real estate. He lost a great deal to the fire. Moreover, his one son (he also had four daughters) had died at the same time. For two years Spafford, who was a friend of evangelist Dwight L. Moody, assisted the homeless, impoverished and grief-stricken who were ruined by the fire.

After two years of gracious work, Spafford and his family decided to take a vacation. They were to go to England to join Moody and Ira Sankey on one of their evangelistic crusades. Horatio Spafford was delayed by some business, but sent his family on ahead. He would catch up with them on the other side of the Atlantic.

Their ship, the Ville de Havre, never made it. Off the coast of Newfoundland, it collided with the English sailing ship, Loch Earn, and sank within 20 minutes. Though Horatio's wife, Anna, was able to cling to a piece of floating wreckage (one of 47 survivors among hundreds), their four daughters Maggie, Tanetta, Annie and Bessie drowned.

Horatio received a distressful telegram from his wife, containing just two words: "Saved alone." Spafford boarded the next available ship to be near his grieving wife. When they met with Dwight Moody, Spafford told him quietly, "It is well. The will of God be done."

Though reports vary as to when he did so, that belief led Spafford to write the words to one of our best-known hymns. Some say he wrote it on the ship to meet his wife, around the place where his daughters died.

It Is Well With My Soul

"When peace, like a river, attendeth my way,
When sorrows like sea billows roll;
Whatever my lot, Thou has taught me to say,
It is well, it is well, with my soul."

How many of us would react like Horatio Spafford? How long would it take to find peace in the midst of such a great loss? Spafford had a relationship with his Savior that neither material nor personal loss could diminish. His countenance must have been one of peace and strength as he met his grieving wife and continued with Dwight Moody. He had a positive effect on those around him—and countless others by the words he wrote. I pray that you will always be able to say, "It is well with my soul."

> *Spread love everywhere you go. Let no one ever come to you without leaving happier.*
>
> —Mother Teresa

Reflections for Discussion

1. Discuss important considerations regarding the needs of the caregiver.

2. What does an attitude of gratitude imply?

3. You have probably encountered a negative person. Describe your feelings while being in their company.

4. What does it mean when you enter a spiritual dry spell?

5. How many of us would react like Horatio Spafford?

6. How long would it take to find peace in the midst of such a great loss?

SEVENTEEN

Never, Never, Never Give Up!

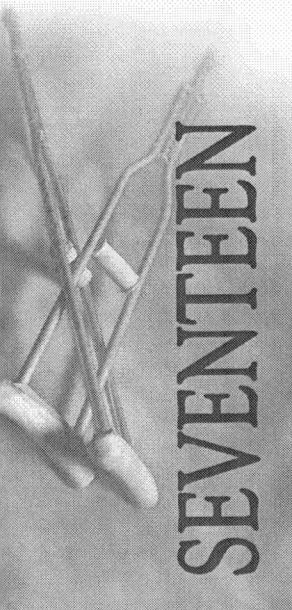

"Anyone who does not believe in miracles is not a realist."

—David Ben-Gurion

How then shall we live?

Winston Churchill delivered a one-line speech to a university commencement. In five words, he gave the best advice and encouragement anyone could ever conceive: "Never, never, never give up." Winston Churchill was born on November 30, 1874 and died on January 24, 1965. During his life of 90 years, he experienced rejection and acceptance. He faced the most difficult times of the 20th century with an attitude of a winner. Defeat was not mentioned in his speeches or in his actions. He carried the weight of a nation and the freedom of Europe on his shoulders. Many people would cave in under such times of stress and burden. I am amazed at the fortitude of people that

God places in leadership over great nations. If a man were to attempt to carry a similar load of responsibility without God's support, he would become a dictator and would lead by fear.

A person with a disability or debilitating illness has a choice: either give up and live in fear and defeat, or stay in the race and win a crown of life.

> "Blessed is the man that endureth temptation: for when he is tried, he shall receive the crown of life, which the Lord hath promised to them that love him" (James 1:12, KJV).

Strong's Concordance describes temptation in this scripture "by implication *adversity.*" It is not the particular adversity that makes a person. It is the way it is handled. I do not like to use the word *cope*, because it implies to get by, make out or make do. Enduring is to "carry on through, despite hardships" and to "suffer patiently without yielding."[1] God is interested in your attitude, and so are the people around you. It defines you as a person. A person who endures to the end without complaint is a hero to me.

I do not know Stephen Hawking. However, I do know of him through articles. His mind's ability to theorize and develop new concepts is incredible. Some might put him on par with Albert Einstein. Another uniqueness of Stephen Hawking is that he has ALS, better known as Lou Gehrig's disease. The disease afflicted him in 1974, when he was 32 years old. Confined to an automated wheel chair, he has to speak through artificial electronic aids.

From the Web site, *www.hawking.org.uk*, are his words,

> "The realization that I had an incurable disease that was likely to kill me in a few years, was a bit of a shock. How could something like that happen to me? Why should I be cut off like this? However, while I had been in hospital, I had seen a boy I vaguely knew die of leukemia, in the bed opposite me. It had not been a pretty sight. Clearly there were people who were worse off than me. At least my condition didn't make me feel sick. Whenever I feel inclined to be sorry for myself I remember that boy.
>
> "I have had motor neurone disease for practically all my adult life. Yet, it has not prevented me from having a very attractive family, and being successful in my work. This is thanks to the help I have received from Jane, my children, and a large number of other people and organizations. I have been lucky, that my condition has progressed more slowly than is often the case. But it shows that one need not lose hope."

❝ Courage is not simply one of the virtues, but the form of every virtue at the testing point. ❞

—C.S. Lewis

Franklin Delano Roosevelt

I recall making a defeatist statement over 20 years ago in a Christian doctor's office. I stated that churches do not want a crippled pastor. The doctor replied, "We had a crippled president." Of course, he was referring to the 32nd President of the United States, Franklin Delano Roosevelt.

Born in 1882 at Hyde Park, New York, Franklin Roosevelt attended Harvard University and Columbia Law School. On St. Patrick's Day, 1905, he married Eleanor Roosevelt. He was elected to the New York Senate in 1910. President Wilson appointed him Assistant Secretary of the Navy, and he was the Democratic nominee for Vice President in 1920.

In the summer of 1921, when he was 39, disaster struck. He was stricken with poliomyelitis. Demonstrating indomitable courage, he fought to regain the use of his legs, particularly through swimming. At the 1924 Democratic Convention, he dramatically appeared on crutches to nominate Alfred E. Smith as "the Happy Warrior." In 1928, Roosevelt became governor of New York.

President Roosevelt was in a wheel chair for the rest of his life. Each day began by putting 12 pound braces on each leg. When he appeared in public, there was a strong man at his arm helping him to stand, and when he spoke, one hand was always firmly grasped to a rail or podium.

He was elected president in November 1932, to the first of four terms. By March 1933, there were 13 million unemployed, and most of the banks were closed. When the Japanese attacked Pearl Harbor on December 7, 1941, Roosevelt directed the organization of the nation's manpower and resources for global war. Feeling that the future peace of the world would depend upon relations between the United States and Russia, he devoted much thought to the planning of a United Nations, in which he hoped international difficulties could be settled. As the war drew to a close, Roosevelt's health deteriorated, and on April 12, 1945, while at Warm Springs, Georgia, he died of a cerebral hemorrhage.

From Warm Springs, Georgia, a slow-moving funeral train passed through the rural South to a service in Washington, D.C., then past the now thriving cities of the North, and finally to Hyde Park, N.Y., in the Hudson River Valley, where he was born. Wherever it passed, Americans by the hundreds of thousands stood vigil to witness a momentous passage of one they loved. Men stood with their arms around the shoulders of their wives and mothers. They stood in clusters, heads bowed, openly weeping. They clasped their hands in prayer. A father lifted his son to see the last car, which carried the flag-draped coffin. "I saw everything," the boy said. "That's good," the father said. "Now make sure you remember."

He had been president of the United States for 12 of the most tumultuous years in the life of our nation. For many, an America without Roosevelt seemed inconceivable. He had guided our nation through democracy's two monumental crises—the Great Depression and World War II. Those who watched his coffin pass were the beneficiaries of his nation's victory. Their children would live to see the causes for which he stood—prosperity and freedom, economic justice and political democracy—gather strength throughout the century and come to dominate life in America and in much of the world.[2]

Franklin Roosevelt's crippling illness was to have a major impact on the perceptions of individuals with handicaps, which tended to be very negative. Individuals with physical handicaps were typically kept at home, out of sight, in back bedrooms by families who felt a mixture of embarrassment and shame concerning their presence.

Even physicians tended to look on "cripples" with derision. Because of these attitudes, children with physical disabilities were often barred from attending public schools. Though these negative attitudes were deep-rooted, Roosevelt's image brought forth a limited form of acceptance for those with handicaps, at least as long as they didn't complain and continued their cheerful determination.

Still, the country would certainly not accept a cripple as its president. F.D.R. had no choice but to obscure the extent of his disability from the public. Just two out of the many thousands of photos of Roosevelt show him in his wheelchair, which illustrates the respect of the press. However, to show how the country has grown to accept disabilities throughout the ensuing decades, FDR's monument at the National Mall in Washington, D.C., depicts him sitting in a wheelchair.[2]

In October of 1924, Roosevelt checked into a cottage on the grounds of the decrepit Meriwether Inn at Warm Springs, Georgia, because of reports that the waters there could somehow "cure" paralysis. Soon after arriving, the *Atlanta Journal* published an article titled "Franklin D. Roosevelt Will Swim to Health." The article described the curative effect of Warm Springs, and stated that Roosevelt had received a warm welcome there. It was syndicated and appeared in many papers across the land. Letters came in a deluge addressed to Roosevelt at Warm Springs. Some desperate patients with polio simply packed their bags and set off for warm springs without an invitation or even permission. They were drawn by Roosevelt's example, and he took an instantaneous and genuine interest in them. This was the beginning of Warm Springs' role as a therapeutic center and sanctuary for polio survivors. F.D.R bought the resort 18 months after arriving there. He renovated and expanded it, and Warm Springs became his second home.

President Roosevelt *never gave up*. He did not give in to polio, though he had the burden of a nation in a time of depression and the freedom of the world on his shoulders. He truly was an overcomer.

I hope you will use this book and get excited over what you can do instead of pining over what you cannot do. If you are tired of being useless, then be useful. If you are young, then visualize a future life of fulfillment, success and happiness. If you are like me—over the hump in age—then dream of what can be and strive for its fruition. Once again, I repeat, "Never, never, never give up!"

> *Nine requisites for contented living: Health enough to make work a pleasure. Wealth enough to support your needs. Strength to battle with difficulties and overcome them. Grace enough to confess your sins and forsake them. Patience enough to toil until some good is accomplished. Charity enough to see some good in your neighbor. Love enough to move you to be useful and helpful to others. Faith enough to make real the things of God. Hope enough to remove all anxious fears concerning the future.*

—Johann Wolfgang von Goethe (1749-1832)

Endnotes

[1] *The American Heritage® Dictionary of the English Language*, Fourth Edition Copyright © 2000 by Houghton Mifflin Company.

[2] The White House Web site, history of Presidents, Franklin D. Roosevelt *http://www.whitehouse.gov/history/presidents/fr32.html*

Reflections for Discussion

1. What did Winston Churchill try to convey with his short speech?

2. How has society changed in its view of the crippled and maimed among us since the early part of the 20th century?

3. It is easy to give up. Why is it important to resist the temptation to succumb to our circumstances?

4. "God will not permit any troubles to come upon us, unless He has a specific plan by which great blessing can come out of the difficulty." What did Peter Marshall mean by this statement?

5. Discuss the implications of accepting God's will and never giving up.